Introducing the Bible

by

ALICE PARMELEE

For whatever was written in former days was written for our instruction, that by steadfastness and by the encouragement of the scriptures we might have hope.

Romans 15.4

MOREHOUSE-BARLOW CO., INC.
WILTON, CONN.

The illustrations used on the cover are from bosses on the ceiling of the Cathedral Church of Saints Peter and Paul, Washington, D.C., and are used by permission. Sculpted by Theodore Barbarossa, the bosses depicted have as their subjects *The Baptism of Jesus* and *Jesus Saves Peter from Drowning.*

The Scripture quotations in this book, unless attributed otherwise, are from the Revised Standard Version of the Bible, copyrighted 1946, 1952, and 1957 by the Division of Christian Education of the National Council of the Churches of Christ in the United States of America and used by permission.

Contents

Preface

The aim of this series is to provide readers, teachers, and students with some of the data they need in order to read the Scriptures with informed minds. To comprehend the breadth and depth of God's message to us in this ancient book, faith without knowledge is as inadequate as knowledge without faith. The Bible does not come to meet us, nor does it demand our attention. Because it is a difficult book to read with understanding, time and effort are required to master it. We need clues to follow if we are to discover for ourselves its treasures.

Clues to guide us through the Scriptures have been provided by eminent scholars and by the Church itself. Experts have established its history, explained its meanings, recreated much of its background, and produced ever more accurate and readable translations of its text. Their work forms the basis of this series. In presenting the material, I have tried to be clear, concise, and, above all, accurate.

The English translation primarily used is the Revised Standard Version which preserves the incomparable beauty of the Tyndale-King James tradition of the English Bible in a corrected text and with a modern approach.

This first book of the series surveys the Bible, records the history of its English translations, and gives suggestions about reading it. "The Divine Names" introduces a necessary aspect of serious Bible study, the search for the exact meaning of words. "Familiar Phrases" indicates the extent to which the Scriptures permeate our language. Finally, "Quintessential Verses" is a compilation of key verses that express the basic message of the Bible.

For invaluable help of all kinds graciously given, I want to thank many people too numerous to list here. I would especially mention my sister Mary who helped with every page. To many others, family, teachers, and friends, who, mostly unknowingly, trained me and imparted their values, wisdom, and faith, I give heartfelt thanks.

Alice Parmelee

Abbreviations For the Books of the Bible

Old Testament

Genesis	Gen	Ecclesiastes	Eccles
Exodus	Ex	Song of Solomon	Song
Leviticus	Lev	Isaiah	Isa
Numbers	Num	Jeremiah	Jer
Deuteronomy	Deut	Lamentations	Lam
Joshua	Josh	Ezekiel	Ezek
Judges	Judg	Daniel	Dan
Ruth	Ruth	Hosea	Hos
1 Samuel	1 Sam	Joel	Joel
2 Samuel	2 Sam	Amos	Amos
1 Kings	1 Kings	Obadiah	Obad
2 Kings	2 Kings	Jonah	Jonah
1 Chronicles	1 Chron	Micah	Mic
2 Chronicles	2 Chron	Nahum	Nahum
Ezra	Ezra	Habakkuk	Hab
Nehemiah	Neh	Zephaniah	Zeph
Esther	Esther	Haggai	Hag
Job	Job	Zechariah	Zech
Psalms	Ps	Malachi	Mal
Proverbs	Prov		

Apocrypha

1 Esdras	1 Esd	Letter of Jeremiah	Letter Jer
2 Esdras	2 Esd	Song of the Three Young Men	Song of Three
Tobit	Tob	Susanna	Sus
Judith	Jth	Bel and the Dragon	Bel
Additions to Esther	Addition Est	Prayer of Manasseh	Prayer
Wisdom of Solomon	Wisdom	1 Maccabees	1 Macc
Ecclesiasticus	Ecclus	2 Maccabees	2 Macc
Baruch	Bar		

New Testament

Matthew	Mt	2 Thessalonians	2 Thess
Mark	Mk	1 Timothy	1 Tim
Luke	Lk	2 Timothy	2 Tim
John	Jn	Titus	Tit
Acts of the Apostles	Acts	Philemon	Philem
Romans	Rom	Hebrews	Heb
1 Corinthians	1 Cor	James	Jas
2 Corinthians	2 Cor	1 Peter	1 Pet
Galatians	Gal	2 Peter	2 Pet
Ephesians	Eph	1 John	1 Jn
Philippians	Phil	2 John	2 Jn
Colossians	Col	3 John	3 Jn
1 Thessalonians	1 Thess	Jude	Jude
		Revelation	Rev

Other Abbreviations

A.D.   *Anno Domini* "in the year of our Lord"
B.C.   Before Christ
c.   *circa* "about," used with uncertain dates
KJV   King James Version (Authorized Version)
NAB   New American Bible
NEB   New English Bible
N.T.   New Testament
O.T.   Old Testament
RSV   Revised Standard Version
v., vv.   Verse, verses

How to Look Up Bible References

Jn 3.16 — the Gospel according to John, chapter 3, verse 16.

Mic 6.5,8 — the Book of Micah, chapter 6, verse 5 and verse 8.

2 Cor 5.17–19 — the Second Letter to the Corinthians, chapter 5, verses 17 to 19 inclusive.

Jer 8.7; 9.3 — the Book of Jeremiah, chapter 8, verse 7; and also chapter 9, verse 3.

Mt 5.2–7.28 — the Gospel according to Matthew, chapter 5, verse 2, to chapter 7, verse 28 inclusive.

Mt 5–7 — the Gospel according to Matthew, chapter 5 through chapter 7.

Mk 8.29; Lk 9.20 — the Gospel according to Mark, chapter 8, verse 29; and Luke, chapter 9, verse 20.

Christ Preaching—Rembrandt (c. 1652)

To these sons and daughters of Abraham, representatives of our common humanity, Christ proclaims his Good News.

I

A Survey of the Bible

THE OUTSTANDING ASPECTS

From every point of view the Bible is an extraordinary book. As a history of ancient times it is indispensable. Its stories never fail to interest readers. As literature its superb examples of both prose and poetry are a delight. Its insight into human nature remains astonishingly true. Its primary value, however, consists in its testimony to the reality of God and to his involvement in human life. Two religions are founded upon that which is recorded in this book. Its Hebrew Scriptures (called the Old Testament by Christians) are the written foundation of Judaism, while both the Old Testament and the New Testament have become the sacred book for Christians. Moreover many of the teachings in the Koran, the holy book of Islam, which is the world's third great monotheistic religion, reflect the traditions of the Bible.

The Bible records one of humanity's most important quests into the vast unknown in which we live. Probably it is the most crucial search of all because it involves the questions that haunt our inmost being: Who am I? Why am I here? Is there a God in heaven who cares for me?

1

What is the final goal of life? Are there moral values which have ultimate significance? To these questions the Bible gives convincing answers to those who read in expectancy and faith.

Like us, the people who figure in the Bible lived in an inscrutable universe that seemed ruthless and often hostile; nevertheless they became aware of a Presence beyond the range of their finite knowledge. As the theologian Hans Küng has said, "Where others perceived only infinite silence, Israel heard a voice." Listening to this Voice and responding to it quickened Israel's faith in God as the ultimate reality. Eventually the people began to know him as the living God of justice and truth, of compassion, grace, and love. All this is set forth and developed in the Bible and constitutes its chief glory.

Actually, as almost everyone knows, the Bible is really not a single book but a collection of documents, virtually a library of sixty-six (or eighty-one, including the Apocrypha) books printed, and bound together in the thousand or more pages that make up our Bibles. Its various books are grouped in two parts, the older and larger is the Old Testament containing thirty-nine books (supplemented in some traditions by the Apocrypha with its fifteen books or parts of books); the shorter is the New Testament with twenty-seven. (A memory device for these numbers is as follows: *Old* has three letters, *Testament* has nine; three and nine placed side by side give thirty-nine. The three of *New* multiplied by the nine of *Testament* give twenty-seven.)

These sixty-six books contain a great variety of stories, legends, historical records, songs, prayers, law-codes, speeches, prophecies, biographical registers, natural history observations, letters, parables, creeds, liturgies, poems, and much more. Each one of these literary forms conveys, in its own way, some aspect of the life, tradi- tions, and faith of ancient Israel and of the Christian Church.

In addition, the pages of the Bible are enlivened by a long procession of people beginning with Adam and Eve. The majority of them are not fictitious characters but true-to-life people whose names remain part of our heritage. They were born, lived, labored, and died, in common with all humanity. Most of them surely endured the pain and bitterness of life; some of them experienced its glory. They present humanity in its infinite variety from beggars to kings, from fools to prophets, from scoundrels to statesmen, from the silly and the selfish to the saints.

In all its richness of reporting the Bible is alive with human action and it sparkles with conversation. One of its exceptional features is that from first to last we hear people talking *about* God and talking *to* him. They question him, they complain, but above all they pray to him. The Bible also reports those rare instances when people talked *with* God.

Fortunately, the teeming pages of the Bible and its many stories do not fly off in a hundred different directions but are held together by a unifying theme. In a word, this is the reality and power of God and his concern for the ultimate well-being of his children. The Bible declares that the world belongs to God who created it and that he is a living God continually acting in human affairs and guiding them in justice and mercy according to his divine purpose, all the while making himself known in many different ways to men and women. In the end, the New Testament proclaims that through his Son Jesus Christ he brings the supreme revelation of himself to humankind.

A BIRD'S-EYE VIEW OF THE CONTENTS

With the first majestic sentence of Genesis the Bible story opens against the vast panorama of Creation, "In the beginning God created the heavens and the earth." Swiftly the narrative focuses on two people, Adam and Eve, and the early generations of their descendants. Again the focus narrows to a particular person, Abraham, the friend of God. He is chosen to be the father of a special people whom the Lord will bless and through whom the Lord will bless the whole world. For their part the people are called to obey God and be faithful to him. Stories of Abraham's son Isaac, his grandson Jacob, his twelve great-grandsons, and their twelve tribes move rapidly on to Moses. Under his leadership the tribes, transformed by the revelation at Mt. Sinai and the giving of the Law and united by their obedience to the Law, become the holy people of Israel, "the people of the Lord your God" (Deuteronomy 27.9).

They settle in their own land, and eventually under Saul, David, and Solomon establish a kingdom that soon splits asunder. During the period of the great prophets the Northern Kingdom of Israel and the Southern Kingdom of Judah are threatened by powerful neighboring empires who destroy first Israel and then Judah. The people of God, however, do not disappear from history with other small contemporary states, for in this transformation, though they become a subject state, they preserve their unique spiritual life in a theocracy governed by their own religious authorities. For about five hundred years they remain under the domination of the successive masters of the Middle East: Assyria, Babylonia, Persia, Greece, Rome. At this time the major features of Jewish religious life take shape, including the establishment of a canon of sacred writings, beginning with the Books of Moses and later supplemented with the Prophets and the Writings.

From the Christian viewpoint the last transformation of Abraham's heirs takes place with the coming of Christ when the people of God become the world-embracing community of the Christian Church. The old blood-kinship that for centuries had united Abraham's family, the tribal federation, the kingdoms, and the theocratic state of Israel is finally superseded. As the apostle Paul explained in a letter to the Gentiles of Galatia, "You are all one in Christ Jesus. And if you are Christ's, then you are Abraham's offspring, heirs according to promise" (Galatians 3.28–29). To Paul, a one-time Pharisee, the Church *is* "the Israel of God" (Galatians 6.16). One of the collects for the Easter Vigil in the new *Book of Common Prayer* expresses Paul's teaching: "Grant that all the peoples of the earth may be numbered among the offspring of Abraham, and rejoice in the inheritance of Israel, through Jesus Christ our Lord."

Finally, in a vision of jeweled splendor, John the Christian seer beholds, in the ultimate transformation, a new heaven and a new earth where death and mourning and crying and pain are ended and all things are made new. From the throne he hears a great voice announcing the consummation of the long Bible story beyond history and beyond time itself, "Behold, the dwelling of God is with men. He will dwell with them, and they shall be his people, and God himself will be with them" (Revelation 21.3).

THE BIBLE AND HISTORY

Is the historical record running through the Bible trustworthy? Yes it is. Like all historians, those who chronicled Biblical events wrote from their own point of view and that of their era. Sometimes they were misinformed. Sometimes, in their enthusiasm, they exaggerated. They were also biased because their faith had been created by many of the events they recorded. They aimed, however, to report accurately. The purpose of the Old Testament authors was to chronicle events so "that you may know the saving acts of the Lord" (Micah 6.5) and learn the "many and various ways God spoke of old to our fathers" (Hebrews 1.1). The archeologist William F. Albright concluded that the Old Testament "is a most extraordinarily accurate record of human experience." The New Testament authors aimed to record how God "in these last days . . . has spoken to us by a Son" (Hebrews 1.2). Luke's purpose was "to write an orderly account . . . that you may know the truth concerning the things of which you have been informed" (Luke 1.3–4). Israel's faith and that of the Church rested primarily on events, on something that had actually happened. This fact guarantees the essential truth of the Biblical record.

History was important to the Bible authors because they believed it was the scene of God's activity. All that happened to men and nations seemed to them to be part of a spiritual epic in which the hand of God could be clearly seen. They thought of history as moving under the guidance of God along a direct line from creation to a future divine consummation. This belief differed from that of the Greeks and others who viewed history as a series of endlessly recurring cycles, like the revolving seasons of winter, spring, summer, and fall. In moments of despair some people have wondered if history is not merely a succession of chance happenings without any meaning or purpose at all. One pessimistic Biblical writer who was probably influenced by Greek thought wrote, "what has happened will happen again" and "time and chance govern all'' (Ecclesiastes 1.9;9.11,NEB). But these statements are rare in the Old Testament, for it is alive with the vitality and hope of those who believe that God controls people and nations and that history is neither a static system of recurring cycles nor a meaningless flow of random events, but chapters in the evolving divine plan of God. The New Testament which contains Jesus' proclamation, "The kingdom of God is at hand" (Mark 1.15), never wavers in its conviction that God's reign on earth, which was manifest in the coming of Christ, will finally be completely realized.

THE MAKING OF THE OLD TESTAMENT

1. When and How the Books Were Written

The thirty-nine books of the Old Testament were written between about 1200 and 100 B.C. Some of them contain ancient fragments, such as Lamech's Taunt (Genesis 4.23–24), Miriam's Song of Triumph (Exodus 15.21), and the Incantation to the Ark (Numbers 10.35–36). These, which are probably survivals from Israel's early tribal days, became embedded, like fossils in a rock, in later historical works.

For several centuries the leaders of Israel passed on to their people and parents taught their children their tribal legends, myths, laws, history, stories, songs, and traditions. Then, about 950 B.C., someone made a collection of this wealth of oral and written material, fusing its miscellaneous parts into a connected historical narrative. This epic is known among scholars as the J Document.

At about the same time another author recorded the events of King David's reign in a history that is called the Early Source of Samuel or the Court History of David's Reign. It can be read today in 2 Samuel 9–20 and 1 Kings

1-2. Because priests in those days were among the few who could read and write, the author of this early history was probably either Abiathar or Ahimaaz, both of whom were important priests at David's court.

Other early sources in the Old Testament, among which are the so-called E, the D, and the P sources, have been identified by scholars who look for the different points of view and the distinctive styles in the text. All these various sources and materials must have been collected, pieced together, and edited to form a more or less continuous story of the people of Israel as we now read it in the books from Genesis through 2 Kings. The theory about a number of early sources and their later combination explains inconsistencies and repetitions in the Biblical narrative. It solves such puzzles as: why there are two superb stories of creation (Genesis 1.1-2.3 and 2.4-3.24); why Joseph is sold to Ishmaelites in one verse and in the next to Midianite traders (Genesis 37.27-28).

Even in such a short book as Amos, for instance, there are evidences of more than one author. Amos himself prophesied in Israel about 750 B.C., at a time when, far away, the legendary brothers Romulus and Remus were founding Rome. But Amos 9.11-15 is clearly a later addition to Amos's work, for these five verses mention the fall of the royal dynasty of David and the Babylonian exile of a people "plucked up" from their land—events that occurred about a century and a half after Amos lived. Indeed many of the books of the prophets show rather extensive additions and editing.

Instead of being written by a single person, most if not all the Old Testament books thus appear to be compilations that include the work of several writers and also of later editors. In antiquity written material was freely borrowed and revised to suit current needs and ideas. This practice of borrowing cannot be condemned as plagiarism because a literary creation was not regarded as its author's personal property. To use older writings was to rescue them from oblivion. A Biblical book is therefore usually a patchwork of earlier works and some, like Proverbs and Psalms, are quite obviously anthologies.

2. What the Books Looked Like

Though no Old Testament book is known to survive in its author's handwriting, early copies of these works still exist. These are written in pen and ink, on scrolls of thin leather (parchment) or on papyrus. The parchment scrolls were made from the skins of sheep, goats, or calves. First these skins were soaked and scraped, then stretched on a frame and polished with pumice to produce a smooth, durable, writing surface that did not wrinkle easily and retained ink well. Next the skins were sewed together to make a strip ten to twenty or more feet long. Finally the strip was rolled around a stick or spindle like a modern window shade. Two hands were necessary to read such a book—one to unwind the scroll, the other to rewind it on a second stick until the desired column of writing came into view. As only one side of the leather was used, a single Old Testament book usually required a long and therefore bulky roll. Such books were inconvenient, expensive, and difficult to store.

Papyrus scrolls were little better. Papyrus is a tall, aquatic plant that in antiquity grew luxuriantly in the Nile Valley and is frequently depicted on Egyptian tombs, pottery, and jewelry. Stalks of this plant were cut and the rind peeled away to expose the central tissue or pith. This was cut into thin slices that were laid vertically and slightly overlapping one another. On top of the first layer a second series of pith strips was laid at right angles to the first. When the two layers were pressed together, the sap of the plant, which is quite adhesive, glued them firmly together. After being dried and polished with a stone, the smooth surface was ready for use. Scribes preferred to write on the side on which their writing ran along the horizontal fibers. Papyrus sheets glued end to end must have formed the scroll on which Baruch transcribed Jeremiah's prophecy and which King Jehoiakim burned in the brazier (Jeremiah 36).

Papyrus is actually at the root of the derivation of the word *Bible*. The Greek name for the inner pith of the papyrus plant, the substance, as we have noted, from which paper was made, was *biblos*. Greek sailors even gave the nickname Byblos or "papyrus city" to the Phoenician seaport of Gebal where they traded for papyrus. As the Scriptures were a collection of papyrus scrolls or codices, it was natural for the Greek Church in the fifth century to list the holy books under the title *ta biblia*, "the papyrus scrolls" or "the books." The underlying unity of the Scriptures eventually transformed this plural noun into a singular one and the title *Bible* emerged. Used for the first complete English translation of the Scriptures, the one prepared in 1382 by John Wycliffe and his followers, it has been the English title ever since.

Not only were the original books of the Bible different in outward appearance from modern books, but their texts ran continuously without the convenience of verse or chapter breaks. This style persisted until about A.D 1228 when Stephen Langton, teacher at the University of Paris and later archbishop of Canterbury, prepared a Bible with chapter divisions to aid his students.

Numbered verses were not introduced until Bibles began to be printed. The Dominican scholar Sanctes Pagninus in 1528 published the first Old Testament with numbered verses. Robert Estienne (Stephanus), the famous French printer and scholar, is said to have prepared the first New Testament with numbered verses in 1551 during a horseback journey from Paris to Lyons while escaping from the turmoils of the Reformation.

3. How the Old Testament Books are Arranged

The books of the Old Testament are not arranged according to their date of origin but according to their kind, with each book placed in one of the three divisions of the Hebrew Bible. These divisions are: Law, Prophecy, Writings.

The Law consists of the five books of Genesis, Exodus, Leviticus, Numbers, and Deuteronomy. In Jewish tradition these books, which tell the origin of the people of God and record his authoritative laws, are known as the Torah, and the authorship is ascribed to Moses. Christian scholars adopted the Greek name *Pentateuch* (*penta* "five" and *teuchos* "tool" or "book") as a convenient title.

Next come the Prophets, which were subdivided into the Former Prophets and the Latter Prophets. The Former Prophets, so named because these books were believed to have been written by men under the inspiration of God, included the four books of Joshua, Judges, Samuel, and Kings. (Samuel and Kings were later divided into two books each.) The Latter Prophets were also reckoned as four books, namely, Isaiah, Jeremiah, Ezekiel, and the Twelve. This last book was a single scroll containing a collection of the twelve shorter prophetic works from Hosea through Malachi.

The third Old Testament group and the last to be canonized was a miscellaneous collection called the Writings. It included Psalms, Proverbs, Job, Song of Solomon, Ruth, Lamentations, Ecclesiastes, Esther, Daniel, Ezra, Nehemiah, and 1 and 2 Chronicles.

In modern Bibles (other than those published for Jewish use) this ancient arrangement of three groups is changed to four groups: (1) Law, comprising the Pentateuch; (2) History, including the twelve books from Joshua through Esther; (3) Wisdom Literature and the Psalms, consisting of the five books from Job through the Song of Solomon; (4) Prophecy, including the four Major Prophets from Isaiah through Daniel, Lamentations, and finally the twelve Minor Prophets, Hosea through Malachi.

4. The Old Testament Canon

When the ancient Hebrews measured something, they used a tall reed called a *kaneh*, meaning something "straight." This Hebrew word for a simple measuring device came metaphorically to mean "measure," "rule," "standard" and is the derivation of our word *canon*. When we speak of the canon of the Old Testament we mean the standard list of books recognized as genuine or inspired Holy Scripture. This Old Testament list was not completed until Christian times, about A.D. 90, but the process of canonization had begun some seven hundred years earlier.

The idea of a holy book, an inspired book, seems to have originated in 621 B.C. In that year, while carpenters, builders, and masons were repairing the Temple in Jerusalem, the high priest discovered a hidden scroll. When it was taken to the prophetess Huldah for authentication, she declared, "This is the word of the Lord the God of Israel" (2 Kings 22.15 NEB). The scroll, which was possibly the original draft of Deuteronomy, was thus from the beginning regarded as an authoritative message from God and therefore a holy book. It became the first *bible* of the people of Israel and the nucleus of our sixty-six-book Bible.

By the time of Jesus the only books that had been canonized and regarded as sacred were those he referred to as "the law and the prophets" (Matthew 5.17), meaning the Pentateuch and the Former and Latter Prophets.

Though Jesus and his contemporaries often quoted from the Writings, these books were not officially included in the canon of the Hebrew Scriptures until after the fall of Jerusalem when a council of rabbis, meeting in Jamnia in A.D. 90, drew up the final, official list. It included the Law, the Prophets, and the Writings, but excluded a collection of books related to the Old Testament now called the Apocrypha.

THE APOCRYPHA

The fifteen books and parts of books that the Jewish rabbis excluded from the Old Testament were very popular works in their day. Although they were written in Hebrew or Aramaic between 200 B.C. and A.D. 90, they were soon translated into Greek. Before long, they ceased to be read in public assemblies and were put aside. Eventually they were given a Greek name *Apokryphos* "hidden" though they were never actually hidden or considered heretical. Today the Jews exclude the Apocrypha from the Hebrew Scriptures, but in Bibles used by Roman Catholic and Eastern Orthodox Churches, in whole or in part, they are considered an important part of the Old Testament. In other Churches, however, the Apocrypha has been treated like a Cinderella. While English Puritans considered it an unworthy addition to the inspired text and rejected it, readings from the Apocrypha have been included in the Anglican Prayer Book lectionary since 1549. At the time of the coronation of King Edward VII, the Archbishop of Canterbury refused to use a copy of the Scriptures that lacked the

Apocrypha because he considered it a mutilated and imperfect Bible.

Today, because of the modern historical approach to the Bible, the Apocrypha is read as a collection of significant documents reflecting the period preceding the rise of Christianity. Two excellent translations of it have been made, one for the Revised Standard Version in 1957, and the other for the New English Bible in 1970. Despite the occasional crudities and the absence of inspiration in many of its books, parts of the Apocrypha, for example, Judith and Tobit, have literary merit, and some, notably, The Wisdom of Solomon and Ecclesiasticus, have unquestioned spiritual value.

THE MAKING OF THE NEW TESTAMENT

1. How the Books Originated

The earliest New Testament book is believed to be Paul's First Letter to the Thessalonians, written from the great port city of Corinth in Greece about A.D. 50. This gentle communication with its hope and thanksgiving is far different from Lamech's shout of revenge, which is possibly the earliest fragment in the Old Testament. Besides this oldest New Testament Letter, Paul wrote others to interpret his faith and to give practical help to local churches struggling with their problems, but he probably never realized that one day his Letters would be considered Holy Scripture.

The same was doubtless true of the writers of the Gospels and the other New Testament books. The earliest Gospel, that of Mark, is dated about A.D. 70, after the deaths of Peter and Paul. The Gospel of Mark, as well as those of Matthew, Luke, and John, appear to be collections of oral and written testimony and tradition concerning Jesus Christ compiled and written to deepen the faith of the particular Christian community for which each was written. Obviously none of the four was intended to supplement the other three or to be read alongside them, and certainly the writers did not consider their work to be Holy Scripture.

2. What the New Testament Books Looked Like

The original New Testament books must have looked like those of the Old Testament because they were also written with pen and ink on parchment or papyrus scrolls, though some of the shorter Letters required only a sheet or two of these materials. When Paul sent an important Letter he dictated it to a secretary (Romans 16.22), usually adding a greeting in his own handwriting (1 Corinthians 16.21; Colossians 4.18).

In the 1st century A.D. a new book form appeared, the codex. This ancestor of the modern book had separate pages instead of being a long, continuous strip. The name *codex*, derived from the Latin *caudex* "tree trunk" or "wooden tablet", hints at its origin. The Greeks and Romans wrote with a metal stylus on wooden tablets coated with a thin layer of wax. The tablets were stacked one on another and bound together by a string threaded through holes along one side. Eventually, instead of using stacks of wooden tablets, the Romans substituted parchment sheets on which they wrote with carbon ink. Paul used such parchment notebooks. When he asked Timothy to bring the cloak he had left at Troas, he also instructed him to bring "the books and above all the parchments" (2 Timothy 4.13). From these rough parchment notebooks some ingenious person invented the codex made from papyrus or parchment. Because most of the oldest-surviving codices are Christian manuscripts, Christians are often credited with inventing this new book form.

A codex, like a modern book, consisted of a stack of quires, each of which was a set of uniform sheets of papyrus or parchment folded inside each other like a pamphlet. The quires were held together by stitching along their folded edges. The advantage of the codex over the scroll was that one could turn its pages instead of unrolling a bulky scroll. Furthermore, both sides of the papyrus or parchment could be written upon, thus reducing by half the amount of writing material required for the same book. While the Jews clung to their traditional scrolls, the Christians quickly adopted the codex. This new mode of communication undoubtedly became a factor in the rapid spread of Christianity. Important papyrus codices copied as early as about A.D. 200 have come to light. These include three Chester Beatty New Testament codices, one of which is a collection of portions of Paul's Letters; and the Bodmer Papyri of Geneva, Switzerland, which include the earliest-known copy of the Gospel of John (though the material after Chapter 14 is fragmentary).

The more brittle papyrus was later replaced by durable parchment, the finest quality of which was vellum. There survive from the fourth century two important vellum codices of the entire Greek Bible, including apocryphal books: Codex Vaticanus in the Vatican Library, and Codex Sinaiticus, fragmentary in the first part of the Old Testament, now in the British Library, London. These two ancient manuscripts together provide the basis for much of the Bible text.

3. The New Testament Canon

The first Bible of the Church was the Old Testament. When Paul instructed Timothy to "devote your attention to the public reading of the scriptures" (1 Timothy 4.13,

NEB), he referred, of course, to the Old Testament because the New Testament documents were still being written.

The Letters of Paul himself were undoubtedly the earliest writings to emerge as sacred scripture. Early in the second century, a Christian author had evidently read a collection of these letters, because he discusses what Paul wrote "in all his letters" (2 Peter 3.16). This apparently indicates that Paul's works, collected, published, and read in churches throughout the Mediterranean world, had already become the nucleus of what would be the Christian Scriptures.

About the same time, the four Gospels, because of their primary witness to the life, death and Resurrection of Jesus, joined Paul's Letters. In recording Church practices, the second–century Christian philosopher Justin Martyr states that passages from "the memoirs of the apostles, which are called gospels" were usually read liturgically in the churches, sometimes instead of the customary readings from Old Testament prophets. Thus the Gospels began to take on the character of Holy Scripture.

During the great flowering of Christian literature in the second century, many gospels were written in support of a wide variety of special and even heretical points of view. But the Church sifted this mass of material and eventually decided that the four Gospels we now read were definitive expressions of the Christian faith as taught by the apostles.

It was many years before the other books of the New Testament were accepted by the whole Church because Christians weighed the value and argued about the inspiration of a wide variety of Christian writings. Of each document people asked such questions as, "Is it historically authentic?" "Do its teachings belong in the mainstream of the Christian faith?" "Was it written by an apostle?"

Finally, twenty-seven books were chosen and canonized, not by any group of experts or an ecclesiastical publication committee, but by the united voice of the Church after several centuries of use and debate.

The earliest list of the New Testament canon as it exists today is found in the Easter letter sent by Athanasius, patriarch of Alexandria, to his clergy in A.D. 367. This prominent Church Father explained that these are the "books that are canonized and handed down to us and believed to be divine."

4. The Arrangement of the New Testament Books

These books are classified as: Gospels, History, Letters, and Apocalypse.

First come the four Gospels, Matthew, Mark, Luke, and John, which provide the basic information about Jesus Christ and his meaning for humankind.

History is represented by the Acts of the Apostles, which covers the period from the forty days following the Resurrection of Jesus through Paul's two years in Rome.

The twenty-one Letters include nine or ten of Paul's, the rest of the Letters and other works being attributed to various early leaders.

In the Christian apocalypse called Revelation, John's poetic vision brings the New Testament to a close on a note of triumph.

5. The Reliability of the New Testament

A modern notion that the New Testament may be little more than a collection of myths fabricated by excited, deluded people does not stand up under a careful reading of the books. The realism found in the first three Gospels with their often down-to-earth touches, the obvious sincerity and deeply felt testimony in the writings, and the basic consistency of the portrait of Jesus sketched by all the authors are evident on every page. If the accounts had been invented primarily for the purpose of propaganda, their contradictions would surely have been corrected. The very inconsistencies in the reports of the Resurrection, for instance, reflect the amazement and incredulity of the many witnesses and make these accounts far more convincing than if they had been in perfect agreement. In contrast to the magic world of make-believe that largely dominates the later apocryphal gospels and epistles, which were excluded from the canon, the canonical books present a believable and living world of men and women whose experiences have the authentic ring of truth.

A COMPARISON OF THE OLD
AND NEW TESTAMENTS

Testament, the word common to the titles of both parts of the Bible, means a binding agreement or covenant between God and humankind. The idea of a covenant is basic to both Old and New Testaments. In the Old Testament the word refers to the covenant God established with Abraham and later renewed under Moses with the whole people of Israel at Sinai: "I will walk among you and will be your God, and you shall be my people" (Exodus 19.6). This covenant is the keynote of the Old Testament. Paul indeed speaks of the Old Testament Scriptures themselves as the old covenant (2 Corinthians 3.14).

The New Testament covenant is that which God re-established through Christ with his people, the Church. At the Last Supper Jesus said, "This cup is the new covenant in my blood" (1 Corinthians 11.25). Christ himself is referred to as "the mediator of a new covenant" (Hebrews 9.15).

The Old Testament, records the two thousand-year history of a vigorous, articulate people. The New Testament, on the other hand, focuses on one person, Jesus Christ, and the first seventy years of the Church.

The heart of the Old Testament consists of its first five books, the Pentateuch. The Four Gospels comprise the heart of the New Testament. Both Pentateuch and Gospels record and interpret actual historical events that were understood, in one case by the prophets and in the other case by the apostles, as God's revelation of himself to his people. The Pentateuch conveys this revelation by means of the early history of Israel; the Gospels, by the birth, ministry, death, and Resurrection of Jesus Christ.

Both the Pentateuch and the Gospels echo with many voices: sometimes two, three, or even four different writers record the same event. Details of these overlapping accounts frequently vary or are contradictory, depending on the writer's distance from the event or his particular point of view. In the Pentateuch the various reports have been fitted together, thus achieving the effect of one continuous story. The Four Gospels, on the other hand, are placed side by side as four separate and distinct books, their individual testimony and view-points being preserved from the repeated editing that submerged the sources of the Pentateuch.

Many Jews, despite the fact that the New Testament is not included in their Holy Scriptures, nevertheless study its record because Jesus was one of their own and in the line of their ancient prophets. Moreover, they appreciate the fact that much of Israel's spiritual heritage reached Western civilization through the New Testament and the Christian Church.

For their part, Christians include the Old Testament in their Bible because they regard it as the cradle of Christianity. Jesus himself was nurtured in the Hebrew Scriptures and frequently quoted from them. When his disciples failed to understand the nature of his mission, he "began with Moses and all the prophets, and explained to them the passages which referred to himself in every part of the scriptures" (Luke 24.27, NEB; cf. John 5.39). The Old Testament is thus regarded as the preparation for and the prelude to God's revelation of himself to his people in Jesus Christ.

THE BIBLE OUTLIVES THE CENTURIES

By the year A.D. 150 all the books of the Old and New Testaments had been written. Could this great and varied collection of sacred writings survive the erosions of time during the next eighteen hundred years? Handwritten texts on parchment and papyrus turn to dust; languages grow and change; people become impatient with old ideas and search for new thoughts. Would the Bible end its life on a shelf of crumbling, unreadable scrolls and codices? Or would the Scriptures reach the twentieth century still capable of stirring the minds and imaginations of men and women and kindling their faith?

1. Papyrus, Parchment, and Printed Paper

Durable though papyrus and parchment are for a short time under favorable conditions, they eventually decay. Yet it was to these materials that the Bible text, laboriously copied in pen and ink for many centuries, was entrusted. Copies were made by the publishing houses of antiquity to satisfy the growing market for the Christian Scriptures. A battery of scribes seated at desks transcribed the words while a reader dictated from the master copy. By this method ten or twenty copies could be made at a time, but they were very costly. During the Middle Ages monks worked alone in their cells or in the drafty cloisters of their monasteries slowly making manuscript copies of the sacred books. By these inefficient ways the Scriptures survived for centuries until paper made of flax or hemp was perfected and printing, invented in the fifteenth century, began to send out its millions of copies.

2. Textual Accuracy

The early centuries of handcopying were the most hazardous for the accuracy of the New Testament text and its faithfulness to the actual words set down by its authors. Before the books were canonized, a copyist might try to improve the sense of an obscure passage or possibly a church leader would alter the meaning of a sentence to make it conform to current doctrine. Scribes, working in haste or experiencing a brief lapse of attention, sometimes introduced careless errors that would then be reproduced in hundreds of subsequent copies. By patiently comparing the surviving early New Testament manuscripts, textual scholars are now able to identify the variant readings. After highly technical study, they then reconstruct a text that is as close to the original one as possible. It is estimated that some two hundred thousand variant readings exist in the thousands of known manuscripts. Fortunately the majority of different readings involve such relatively inconsequential matters as spelling, grammar, or obvious scribal inaccuracies. Not one of the many variants has been found to affect any important New Testament teaching.

With the Hebrew text the story is different. After the Romans obliterated the Jewish state in A.D. 70, destroying

Jerusalem and the great Temple, all hope seemed gone. "Zion has been taken from us and we have nothing now but the Mighty One and his Law," cried one of the Jews appalled by the apparent loss of all that made them a people. But treasured scrolls of the Scriptures were rescued from the burning city and survived to become the very heart of Judaism. Schools were established in which young men learned to read and preserve every word of the sacred text, which now became the "portable fatherland" of the Jews.

Hebrew scrolls enshrining their faith in the Lord were carefully copied lest one word of God to his people be lost. Copyists wrote nothing from memory but read and pronounced each word of the original before writing it in their copies and proofreaders regularly destroyed any page upon which they found two errors.

It is mainly to the Jewish scholars known as Masoretes (from the Hebrew word meaning "tradition") that the careful preservation of the Hebrew text is due. These scholars, who lived in the centers of Jewish culture and learning from the sixth to the tenth centuries, not only standardized the text but devised a system of signs to indicate vowels. Because ancient Hebrew was written solely in consonants, each generation of scribes and scholars, after being taught the precise word indicated by the consonants, had to memorize its pronunciation. All this changed after the Masoretes "pointed" the consonantal text. The Masoretic text has been the basis of English versions of the Bible. Our modern versions used the Masoretic text of the Ben Asher family of scholars as this is preserved in the Leningrad Codex transcribed in 1008. The discovery of the Dead Sea Scrolls beginning in 1947 produced portions of all of the Old Testament books (except Esther) and a complete scroll of Isaiah. These are now the oldest extant manuscripts of the Hebrew Scriptures and are available to us for checking and correcting the accuracy of the Masoretic text.

3. The Book of a Thousand Tongues

The barrier of an unknown language, a frequent obstacle to the communication of a message, has time after time been overcome by devoted translators in the service of the Bible. Between 250 and 100 B.C. the original Hebrew text of the Old Testament, with its few Aramaic sections, was translated into Greek for the Greek-speaking Jewish community living in Egypt whose members no longer understood the Scriptures read to them in Hebrew. This first Bible version is known as the Septuagint, meaning "seventy." Any translation of the original languages of the Bible—of the Hebrew text of the Old Testament, or the Greek text of the New Testament—is called a version.

The name *Septuagint* refers to its seventy legendary translators, who, according to a picturesque story, were invited by the Egyptian ruler Ptolemy II (285–246 B.C.) to translate the Pentateuch into Greek for his famous library in Alexandria. The scholars came from Jerusalem—six from each tribe—and each man worked independently for seventy days. Then, completing their task at the same moment, they shouted "Amen" in unison and all their translations were found to be identical! The Septuagint contained many of the books which were later called the Apocrypha, as well as those later pronounced canonical by the Palestinian rabbis.

After the other Old Testament books were rendered into Greek, not only the Jews of Egypt but those living in other Greek-speaking cities could hear their Scriptures read in a language they understood. The Septuagint became the Bible of the early Church and it was from this version that most of the New Testament authors usually quote. Partly because of this, the Jews later repudiated the Septuagint and used other Greek translations.

The books of the New Testament were written in the Greek language, though some of the sources used by their authors must have been in Aramaic, the language of Jesus and his disciples. (Traces of the Aramaic words actually spoken by Jesus can still be found in Matthew 27.46; Mark 5.41; 7.34; 14.36.) The first Christian Bible, however, in both its parts was a Greek book. Because the Church remained predominantly Greek-speaking for its first two centuries, the surviving earliest Christian manuscripts of the Scriptures are almost all written in that language.

When Latin became the official language of the Roman Empire, the Church gradually adopted it and by A.D. 250 several Latin translations were in use. These are called the Old Latin versions to distinguish them from Jerome's stately new Latin version completed about A.D. 400 and known as the Vulgate. The Vulgate became the principal Bible of Western Europe for a thousand years and from the fifth century to the Reformation its words were read, sung, spoken in prayer, and patiently copied in thousands of manuscript books. It inspired theology, literature, learning, and great works of art from the beginning of the Middle Ages through the Renaissance. When the invention of moveable type brought an end to the handcopying of books, the first substantial book ever printed was the Vulgate. This is the famous Gutenberg Bible of about 1455.

As Christianity spread, other peoples needed copies of the Scriptures in their native or mother tongues. These vernacular versions of early times are in such languages as Aramaic, Syriac, Coptic, Armenian, Georgian, Ethiopic, Arabic, Gothic, Slavonic. For the Armenian Bible an alphabet had to be devised because up to that time nothing had been written in that tongue. The Gothic Bible is the oldest surviving piece of literature in any Teutonic language. For the black people of Abyssinia, a Bible in their classical Ethiopic language was translated a thousand years before John Wycliffe and his followers prepared the first complete English version in 1382. Textual scholars value ancient copies of these very early versions because they indicate the wording of the parent Hebrew and Greek texts before successive handcopying had introduced errors.

Translators since the Reformation have not only kept pace with the rise of national languages in Europe, but they have continued to produce new versions as these languages have changed and developed. In modern English alone there are at least six complete and scholarly versions. With more areas of the world coming into the orbit of Christianity, devoted people translate the Bible into the language of these areas so that the title *The Book of a Thousand Tongues* is already obsolete. By 1978 there was a list of 1,631 languages and dialects into which the entire Bible or parts of it had been translated.

4. The Bible and the Arts

The Bible not only speaks in many languages but its message has been presented through the centuries by all the arts. Music was a handmaid to the Scriptural text from the beginning, enhancing and interpreting its words in various musical compositions from chants, hymns, and spirituals to such superb works as the *St. Matthew Passion* by J.S. Bach and *The Messiah* by G.F. Handel.

Drama as represented by miracle and mystery plays of the Middle Ages spread knowledge of the Bible among the common people. Cycles of these plays on Scriptural themes ranging from Creation to the Second Coming were acted with great gusto by members of the medieval town guilds. A number of these have been collected and published in modern editions.

The visual arts have also used the Scriptures as a source book, depicting many Biblical events and people in a great variety of media from paint to the modern moving picture. Artists have decorated churches and cathedrals to inspire devotion and communicate faith. They have carved in wood and stone; designed mosaics; drawn and painted upon walls, canvas, and paper; fashioned storytelling windows from pieces of colored glass; fabricated objects from metal; worked with enamel; and illuminated hundreds of Bible manuscripts with exquisite miniature paintings that, like enchanted windows, open up the holy text itself. From the beauty, order, and deep seriousness of all these works the beholder not only gains insight into the artist's own faith, but catches a reflection of the divine glory.

It is characteristic of artists to portray the people and events of the Bible in terms of the customs, dress, and outlook of their own era, recording, often with great understanding and fidelity, the outwardness of the story, but inevitably stamping it with the indelible mark of the particular period in which the work of art was created. Some of the supreme artists, such as Giotto, Fra Angelico, Botticelli, Leonardo da Vinci, Michelangelo, Raphael, Titian, El Greco, and Rembrandt, often achieved even more. By means of line, form, color, and design, master artists somehow, transcending the limitations of their own day and the surface appearance of things, appeal directly to our inner eye and convey the real but invisible dimension of our life in God.

THE BIBLE TODAY

Today our knowledge and understanding of the Bible have been greatly increased through the devoted and continuing labors of many people. Scholars, employing modern techniques of historical, textual, and linguistic research, have produced a Hebrew and a Greek text closer to the original words of the Biblical authors than ever before. Translators, working from these texts, have provided us with more accurate and more easily readable versions than were formerly available. Scholarly exegetes, whose function is to explain and interpret, annotate our Bibles using not only today's scientific and historical insights but the comments of former generations.

Until the beginning of the nineteenth century, the world in which Abraham, Moses, David, Jesus, and Paul lived was virtually unknown. Except for the Scriptures themselves, with some additional information gleaned from Greek and Latin authors and a few facts brought back from the Crusades, the ancient Middle East had all but vanished. Today, however, the world of the Bible speaks to us in a multitude of voices and is vividly and authentically known in many of its aspects. Archaeologists identify Biblical sites, excavate buried structures, and interpret the meaning of the artifacts they unearth. Travellers and photographers describe and take pictures of almost every corner of the region. Geographers and other scientists survey its physical features and catalogue its many forms of life. Historians, sociologists, and others reconstruct the social life of ancient Israel and the primitive church from all available evidences of their institutions, customs, and ways of living.

Thus it has come about that in our modern world the Bible, far from being a literary fossil, is more alive than ever, as the millions of copies issuing from the printing presses each year testify. No one progresses far in the study of literature or art without a detailed knowledge of the Bible. The almost daily allusions to it in the media are incomprehensible to those who have no acquaintance with its stories and its personalities. Whether we know it or not, we often speak in Biblical phrases, as will be evident by glancing at a later section entitled "Familiar Phrases from the English Bible."

Now that our approach to the Scriptures has changed from one that was inclined to be indiscriminating and uncritical to one that is based on historical and scientific knowledge and that uses comparative standards of analysis, more people than ever before are reading the Bible with understanding and searching for its living message. As always before in history, a sincere and intelligent effort to grasp this message brings us near to the life-enhancing and sustaining reality of God.

Copyright photograph © British and Foreign Bible Society, London

The Last Chapter—J. Doyle Penrose (1902)

Just before his death in 735 the Venerable Bede, in his Northumbrian monastery, finishes his translation of John's Gospel into Anglo-Saxon.

II

The Bible in English

OLD ENGLISH AND MIDDLE ENGLISH VERSIONS
A.D. 650–1350

The story of the Bible in English begins in the great abbey of Whitby in Yorkshire, England, founded in 658 by the Northumbrian princess Hilda. Among those she employed on the farms was an illiterate cowherd named Caedmon. According to the Venerable Bede's *Ecclesiastical History of the English People*, one night in a dream Caedmon was miraculously given the gift of poetry and song. The steward of the abbey, hearing Caedmon sing a hymn he had composed, took him to the Abbess Hilda. She tested his gift by teaching him a passage from the Latin Bible which he immediately transformed into a matchless poem in his native tongue of Old English. All who heard it agreed that the grace of God was upon Caedmon. Abbess Hilda received him into the abbey as a lay brother and directed the monks of this famous center of Christian learning to teach him the Bible. He then phrased its stories in "most delightful poetry," for he aimed "to turn men from wickedness and help them love righteous living."

Caedmon's poems were not translations but paraphrases; not written but sung; and not in modern English,
a language that would emerge many centuries later, but in
Old English, also called Anglo-Saxon. His works are,
nevertheless, the earliest known attempts to express the
Bible message in a language that the great mass of illiterate
people of Britain could understand. Though only a few
lines of his work survive, Caedmon himself is com-
memorated at Westminster Abbey in the Poets' Corner by
a paving stone inscribed simply with his name and the
tribute, "who first among the English made verses."

Aldhelm, abbot of Malmesbury, like his contemporary
Caedmon, used music to attract an audience to the Biblical
message, for he saw that his listeners were not interested
in his sermons. The abbot would go out on the highway
dressed as a minstrel and play upon his harp until a crowd
of passers-by assembled. Then he would sing about
Scriptural themes and thus win many to Christianity.
Later, when he was bishop of Sherborne, he made the
first-known translation of the Psalms into Anglo-Saxon.

The Venerable Bede (673–735), the most renowned
Christian scholar of the eighth century, was a monk of the
joint monastery of Wearmouth and Jarrow in North-
umbria. He has been called "the father of English learning" because his forty works, mostly in Latin, spanned
the whole field of knowledge of his day and were used by
students in monastic schools throughout Europe. His
Ecclesiastical History of the English People is the chief
source for the first eight centuries of Christian history in
the British Isles. Because, as he explained, "I do not want
my boys (monks) to read ... to no purpose after I am
gone," this gentle, heroic scholar prepared Anglo-Saxon
translations for them, finishing his rendering of John's
Gospel only upon his deathbed. No trace of his final work

remains, for it was probably swept away with other Northumbrian treasures during the Danish invasions.

The earliest surviving example of an Anglo-Saxon translation inserted between the lines of the Latin text of the Psalter is the Vespasian Psalter which is now in the British Library, London. This interlinear gloss was written in Mercia c. 825.

Beginning with the tenth century, Anglo-Saxon translations of portions of the Scriptures multiplied. King Alfred prefaced his code of laws with the Ten Commandments and other Biblical laws. He himself is said to have translated some of the Psalms. The priest Aldred, later Bishop of Durham, inserted a paraphrase in the Northumbrian dialect between the lines of the Lindisfarne Gospels, a magnificently illuminated, seventh-century Latin manuscript, now one of the treasures of the British Library, London. Aldred's gloss, dating from c. 950, is the earliest-known version of the Gospels in Old English. Its Old English translation inserted above the Latin words of the Matthean version of the Lord's prayer reads:

> fader urer ou aro ou bist in heofnum in heofnas
> Pater noster qui est in caelis

Independent Anglo-Saxon Gospels, unaccompanied by the Latin text, soon began to appear. No fewer than six manuscripts of these readable, complete, and accurate translations in the West Saxon dialect survive, two each in the libraries of Oxford and Cambridge, and in the British Library of the British Museum, London.

Aelfric, c. 955–1020, a scholarly monk of Winchester and later abbot of Eynsham near Oxford, is doubtless the most important figure in the history of the English Bible before Wycliffe. His work consists of the earliest extant English version of the narrative books of the Old Testament. In his clear, fluent Old English style he was a prolific writer, producing, among other works, three books of homilies or sermons containing Old Testament translations and passages from the New Testament. His aim, as stated in one of his prefaces, was to convey religious instruction in simple English for the benefit of those who did not know Latin. He had misgivings, however, "lest peradventure the pearls of Christ be had·in disrespect." But "the request of many of the faithful . . . and particularly that of the earl Aethelwold" (a patron of learning and son of the founder of Eynsham Abbey), encouraged him to complete his paraphrase of the Pentateuch and Joshua, parts of which he did not consider suitable for simple minds. He also wrote epitomes or summaries of Kings and Job and translations of Esther, Judith, and Maccabees. The last three were probably intended to raise the fighting spirit of the English during the Danish invasions. "At this time," Aelfric wrote, "much more knowledge is necessary for laymen, because all the world is far spent in its manifold miseries."

After the Norman conquest of 1066, the king decreed that Old English should be suspended in favor of the French spoken by the conquerors. Soon the upper classes began to speak a strange hybrid of French and Old English called Anglo-Norman. Local schoolmasters, country priests, monks, and peasants, however, clung to their accustomed language. During the Anglo-Norman period, extending into the early fourteenth century, no more Old English Bibles were produced because Anglo-Norman reigned supreme. But, following the victories of Edward III and the Black Prince over the French in the Hundred Years' War, an English national spirit reawakened among the people. More and more they looked upon French as a foreign tongue and a new English language began to emerge. It was based upon the old Anglo-Saxon, but enriched by French words of the Norman conquerors and Latin words from the Vulgate. This new language, known as Middle English, was popularized by such works as Chaucer's *Canterbury Tales*, two new versions of the Psalms, and finally Wycliffe's Bible. A speech in Middle English opened the Parliament of 1399.

The two versions of the Psalms were the anonymous *Midland Psalter*, c. 1325; and *Richard Rolle's Psalter*, c. 1340. Richard Rolle, after studying religion at Oxford, returned to Yorkshire where he was known as the hermit and mystic of Hampole. He wrote many treatises and devotional works in Latin and English. According to the preface of his *Psalter*, he undertook the translation into Middle English at the request of a woman he had healed, "a werthy recluse . . . cauld dame Merget Kyrkby," to whom he dedicated some of his works. The popularity and wide circulation of these Psalters was an important factor in the triumph of the new English language over competing languages and dialects. Now that the Psalms existed in a version people could easily understand, they began to seek further knowledge of the Scriptures.

THE WYCLIFFE BIBLE, 1382

Seven hundred years after Caedmon sang his paraphrases, the first complete version of the English Bible appeared. This landmark translation was a direct result of the teachings of John Wycliffe (c. 1320–1384). He was the most eminent Oxford theologian of his day, a man of considerable political and ecclesiastical importance and a master of the new English language. Wycliffe deplored the ignorance and superstition that had led to corruption in the Church. On the basis of his belief that all who disregard God's law are automatically dispossessed of the power and dominion they derive from God, he challenged the supremacy of the pope and his final authority over English ecclesiastical and political affairs. The supreme spiritual authority, he argued, an authority higher even than that of the Church or Catholic tradition, is the Bible. It contains God's law and is the very voice of God. According to Wycliffe, everyone must be given access to the Scriptures so that he can discover for himself the only reliable rule of faith and the standard of holiness. To that end he urged that the Bible be translated from Latin, which only the educated and the upper classes could understand, into the common tongue of the English people.

Wycliffe himself became the moving spirit in rendering the entire Vulgate into English. Among the scholars who assisted him was his pupil, a master of theology at Oxford, Nicholas Hereford. Hereford is believed to have translated some of the Latin Old Testament in a very literal, pedantic style, before he was abruptly summoned to London and excommunicated. Wycliffe himself may have translated most of the New Testament. About thirty manuscripts of this complete English Bible of 1382 survive, many of them plain small volumes intended for monastic libraries or private people. A large and handsome two-volume copy now in the British Library, London, originally belonged to Thomas of Woodstock, Duke of Gloucester and youngest son of Edward III. An order of poor preachers called Lollards was organized by Wycliffe to spread his doctrines and circulate the first English Bible among the people.

A thoroughly revised and improved edition of the Wycliffe manuscript Bible of 1382 was soon prepared, probably by Wycliffe's disciple and secretary, John Purvey. Purvey, as he explains in his prologue, enlisted the aid of "divers fellows and helpers . . . cunning at correcting of the translation." So popular did this edition become that about 140 copies survive, most of them pocket volumes for the ordinary person, though some are large, decorated copies which belonged to such personages as Henry VI, Henry VII, Edward VI, and Elizabeth I. The *Word of Truth*, which the enthusiastic citizens of London presented to Queen Elizabeth on her accession to the throne in 1558 and which she gratefully received, is believed to have been a copy of Wycliffe's Gospels.

Church authorities, fearing the spread both of Wycliffe's doctrines and his Bible, imprisoned many of his followers, including Nicholas Hereford and John Purvey, and burned any Bibles they could seize. A Church synod meeting in 1408 forbade anyone, under penalty of excommunication, to translate or even read an English version without permission from a bishop. Nevertheless, the Wycliffe Bible continued to be laboriously copied and eagerly read for the next hundred years.

The Scriptures entered a new era when Johannes Gutenberg introduced the art of printing. His great folio volumes of the Vulgate were printed on his press at Mainz c. 1455. The Gutenberg Bible was the prelude to printing in the West. Printing made possible an increased circulation of the Bible, aided in its textual study, and fostered many new translations in the new languages then emerging in Europe. In Italy the first printed Hebrew text of the Old Testament was published in 1488. Erasmus, the outstanding Dutch humanist, theologian, and scholar, while he was in Cambridge between 1511 and 1514, edited the Greek New Testament text. This was printed by Froben at Basle in 1516 and dedicated to Pope Leo X. The first English printer, William Caxton, set up his press in the almonry of Westminster Abbey as early as 1476, but did not issue the current English Bible version, that of Wycliffe, undoubtedly because it was forbidden by the

Church. Caxton did, however, include the Gospel story and the chief parts of the Old Testament narrative in his translation of the *Golden Legend*, which appeared in 1483. When the first printed English Bible was undertaken it had to be produced abroad.

WILLIAM TYNDALE, FATHER OF THE ENGLISH BIBLE, 1525

Reform of the Church was in the air when William Tyndale studied at Oxford and later at Cambridge, probably under Erasmus, the leading scholar of the Greek New Testament. Erasmus did not employ the time-honored medieval interpretations of Scripture because he planned to rediscover the Bible through a truly historical understanding of its ancient texts. His basic purpose was to use the Scriptures to reform the Church from within. "I totally disagree," he declared, "with those who are unwilling that the Holy Scriptures translated into the common tongue should be read by the unlearned." Fired by this revolutionary idea, Tyndale became indignant when a learned churchman said that it was safer to keep the Bible in Latin and let priests explain it than to make it available to ordinary people. Tyndale replied, "If God spare my life, ere many years I will cause a boy that driveth the plough shall know more of the Scripture than thou doest."

He was as good as his word. Finding it impossible because of the Church's opposition to translate the New Testament anywhere in England, he crossed to the continent. In Hamburg he completed his English version of the New Testament, basing it not on the Latin Vulgate, which was, of course, a translation, but upon the recently-printed Greek text edited by Erasmus. Tyndale's superb command of the emerging modern English language and his scholarly use of the Greek text gave freshness and authority to his version. His first attempt to have it printed at Cologne ended when a group of his printers, their tongues having been loosened with wine, revealed the nature of their work to the authorities. Fearful that his translation would be confiscated, Tyndale seized the quarto sheets already printed and fled by boat up the Rhine to Worms. There in 1525 at Peter Schoeffer's press 3,000 copies of the first printed English Scripture were successfully produced in an octavo edition.

Enemies of the Reformation, alarmed that Tyndale was spreading Luther's controversial doctrines by means of the marginal notes in his English New Testament, wrote a letter to Henry VIII warning him to guard his ports against an impending "invasion of England" by this "pernicious merchandise." Though concealed in bales of hay and bundles of flax, many volumes were seized and a bonfire made of them at St. Paul's Cross in London by Bishop Cuthbert Tunstall. Once safely past the authorities, however, the surviving Bibles were eagerly bought and read. Only one complete copy of this first octavo edition is now known to exist. Even this copy, which is in the Baptist College in Bristol, England, lacks a title-page. Of the earlier quarto edition begun at Cologne and completed at Worms, a fragment, Matthew 1.1–22.12, survives and is now in the British Library, London.

In the eleven years of exile that remained to him, Tyndale continued his work. He translated the Old Testament from Genesis to Chronicles, published his Pentateuch, and issued two revisions of his New Testament. The British Library owns Anne Boleyn's handsome vellum copy of his definitive 1534 revision. On its gold edges are inscribed in red letters: *Anna Regina Angliae.* The queen had aided one of the English merchants accused of selling Tyndale's first edition and this presentation copy may have been Tyndale's thanks for the queen's favor.

Because of the treachery of one whom he considered a friend, Tyndale was seized by officers of Emperor Charles V, imprisoned in the cold damp dungeon of Vilvorde Castle near Brussels, and executed for heresy in 1536. His dying prayer was, "Lord, open the king of England's eyes."

Most of the translators who followed Tyndale used his clear and scholarly work as the basis for their versions. Today his simple yet majestic style and the rhythm of his phrases can still be found in the King James Version—ninety percent of its New Testament, it is estimated, comes from him. His phrases and sentences have become part of the texture of English: "the burden and heat of the day"; "eat, drink, and be merry"; "in Him we live, move, and have our being"; "a prophet hath no honor in his own country"; "the powers that be"; "you cannot serve God and mammon"; "consider the lilies of the field how they grow"; "It is more blessed to give than to receive"; "out of darkness into His marvellous light"; and many more. The English Bible undoubtedly owes more to William Tyndale than to any other translator. Moreover, his translations molded the style and character of the English language itself, giving it the fluency, richness, directness, and grace that were to flower in the Elizabethan period. Indeed, even more than Shakespeare and Bunyan, Tyndale shaped and enriched the English language.

SEVEN ENGLISH BIBLES, 1535–1610

Coverdale's Bible, 1535, was the first complete English Bible to be printed. It was prepared by Miles Coverdale,

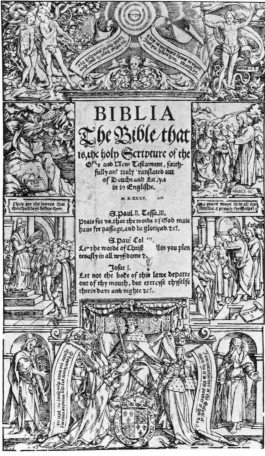

The Pierpont Morgan Library

The Title Page of the Coverdale Bible, 1535

The first complete Bible printed in the English language was prepared by Miles Coverdale and dedicated to King Henry VIII, who is depicted here giving the Bible to his bishops and nobles.

an effective preacher who became chaplain to young
Edward VI and later Bishop of Exeter. Coverdale's Bible,
probably printed in Zurich and imported into England,
was dedicated to, but not authorized by, Henry VIII.
Besides making many translations himself, Coverdale
used the best English versions he could find and also
studied those in other languages. His text contains
phrases of exceptional beauty, especially in the Psalms.
His rendering of these has long been in use, because it was
used in the Great Bible of 1539 and adopted as the Psalter
in the *Book of Common Prayer.*

Matthew's Bible, 1537, the basis of subsequent English
versions, was compiled by John Rogers, Tyndale's friend
and literary executor, from all of Tyndale's translations
and some of Coverdale's. Rogers, in order to conceal his
identity during the years of religious upheavals, published this version under the pseudonym "Thomas Matthew." But he was the first martyr burned at Smithfield,
outside London, in the reign of Mary Tudor.

Taverner's Bible, 1539, is an edition of Matthew's Bible
prepared by Richard Taverner, a layman and graduate of
Oxford. His editorial changes demonstrate his knowledge
of Greek and his gift for writing. To him is owed the
reading, "If any man will come after me, let him deny
himself and take up his cross and follow me."

The Great Bible, 1539, is another revision of Matthew's
Bible, this one edited by Coverdale at the request of
Thomas Cromwell, chief minister of Henry VIII. It is a
handsome folio volume, nine by fifteen inches, with a title
page probably designed by the court painter, Hans Hol-
bein. The first edition is sometimes called "Cromwell's
Bible" because Thomas Cromwell encouraged its publication. The second edition, issued in 1540, is often called
"Cranmer's Bible" because Thomas Cranmer, archbishop
of Canterbury, wrote its preface. Its title page clearly
states "This is the Bible apoynted to the use of the

churches." Seven editions of this immensely popular version, which was without controversial notes, appeared within two years and every clergyman was ordered to set up a copy in his church where parishioners could read it. All day long the six copies chained to the pillars of St. Paul's Cathedral, London, were surrounded by crowds of people reading, arguing, or waiting to read.

The Geneva Bible (New Testament, 1557; complete Bible, 1560), a scholarly revision of earlier versions, was produced by English scholars living as refugees in Switzerland. The chief editor was William Whittingham, an Oxford scholar who was John Calvin's brother-in-law. The Geneva Bible with its marginal notes was the Bible of the reformers John Calvin and John Knox. It became the popular family Bible because it was small, relatively inexpensive, and, for the first time in an English Bible, its chapters were divided into numbered verses. This was the version Shakespeare used and the one taken by the early colonists to America. The Geneva Bible introduced such phrases as: "in all these things we are more than conquerors through Him that loved us", "so great a cloud of witnesses."

The Bishops' Bible, 1568, a revision of the Great Bible, was prepared by Matthew Parker, archbishop of Canterbury, assisted by others. Short, marginal notes of an informative nature were added, but no "bitter notes." Appearing in a magnificent folio volume, it was designated as an official Bible by the Convocation of the Church of England, though it never formally received the queen's official designation as such. It introduced some memorable phrases, among which are: "persecuted for righteousness' sake", "overcome evil with good", "was made in the likeness of men."

The Douay-Rheims Bible (New Testament, 1582; Old Testament in two volumes, 1609 and 1610) was prepared for English-speaking Roman Catholics by a group of

Oxford scholars living in exile in France. Gregory Martin, the chief translator, based his work on the Latin Vulgate which he rendered in such a literal way that his work was described as "a translation that needed to be translated." He did not hesitate, however, to borrow freely from the earlier English versions beginning with that of Tyndale. He also consulted the Greek New Testament text. In this version appear such happy expressions as: "the ministry of reconciliation"; "to me to live is Christ, and to die is gain." The Douay-Rheims Bible was produced to counteract the growing popularity of Protestant Bibles many of which contained notes critical of the Roman Catholic Church. It was not intended for general use because only those "as have expresse licence" were supposed to read it. The makers of the King James Version of 1611, despite the strongly English character of their style, consulted the Rheims New Testament and borrowed some of its Latin flavor to good effect. The Douay-Rheims Bible remained the authorized English version for Roman Catholics until 1750 when Bishop Challoner of London revised the text, chiefly by adopting many renderings from the King James Version. The Challoner-Douay-Rheims Version remained for many years the standard translation for Roman Catholics.

THE KING JAMES VERSION, 1611

The King James Version, also called the Authorized Version, came into being as a result of a conference summoned in 1604 by James I to Hampton Court Palace. The conference was convened to settle difficulties between the bishops of the Church of England and the Puritan Party. As a result of an apparently chance suggestion made by Dr. John Reynolds, president of Corpus

Christi College, Oxford, and leader of the Puritans, a new English version was initiated. Reynolds moved that a new translation of the Bible be made because those then in use he found "corrupt and not answerable to the truth of the original." Taken by surprise at the unexpected proposal, James, a Biblical scholar himself, having translated the Psalms into verse and written a paraphrase of Revelation, quickly agreed to Reynold's motion. He appointed a panel of fifty-four distinguished scholars, including six bishops. They were to use the Bishops' Bible as their basic text and exclude controversial marginal notes. The revisers organized themselves into six groups, two at Westminster, two at Oxford, and two at Cambridge, each group working with its assigned portion of the Scriptures. The Westminster company, which included William Bedwell, the greatest Arabic scholar of Europe, was presided over by Lancelot Andrewes, later bishop of Winchester, who knew so many languages that it was said he "might have been interpreter-general at Babel." The Oxford company included Dr. John Reynolds and Dr. Miles Smith who "had Hebrew at his finger ends." Dr. Smith was the author of the informative preface, entitled "The Translators to the Reader." The Cambridge group included John Bois, chief lecturer in Greek at St. John's College. He read Hebrew at the age of six and wrote letters in Greek at fifteen. Bois was one of the committee of six final revisers who, when the work of translating and editing was complete, went daily for nine months to Stationers Hall, London, to oversee the printing at Robert Barker's press. Each of these six men were paid thirty shillings a week, the only remuneration any of the revisers received.

On the basis of the best Hebrew and Greek texts available to them these learned men produced, not a completely original work, but a scholarly revision of

Tyndale's and succeeding versions. Their purpose was not "to make a new translation . . . but to make . . . out of many good ones, one principal good one not justly to be excepted against." In this they succeeded, crowning nearly a century of translating, editing, and perfecting with a version that became the undisputed English Bible for the simple reason that it was the best.

The translators, experienced as most of them were in reading the Scriptures in public, had acquired a sense of what would sound well when read aloud. Thus they were able, when choosing the final wording, to create a poetic prose of strength and harmony and to maintain a rhythmic flow that gives a sense of the music and majesty of the English language.

Several comparisons with earlier versions illustrate the excellence of the King James Version:

> Matthew's Bible: When the morning stars praised me together, and all the children of God rejoiced triumphantly (Job 38.7).
>
> KJV: When the morning stars sang together, and all the sons of God shouted for joy.
>
> Tyndale: Come unto me all ye that labor and are laden and I will ease you (Mt 11.28).
>
> KJV: Come unto me, all ye that labour and are heavy laden, and I will give you rest.
>
> Coverdale and Matthew: So that they shall break their swords and spears, to make scythes, sickles and saws thereof. From that time forth shall not one people lift up weapon against another, neither shall they learn to fight from henceforth (Isa 2.4).
>
> KJV: They shall beat their swords into plowshares, and their spears into pruninghooks: nation shall not lift up sword against nation, neither shall they learn war any more.

BIBLES FOR TODAY

The King James Version maintains its honored place among Bible readers as probably the most beautiful and influential translation of the Scriptures ever made and certainly one of the supreme monuments of English literature. Through the years its spelling, punctuation, and grammar have been revised to conform to modern usage, but its incomparable text remains basically intact, preserving a numinous quality that is especially evident when the Scriptures are read in public. However, with the passage of time, changes in the English language make the 1611 version seem more and more antiquated. Added to this, discoveries of better Hebrew and Greek texts than those underlying the King James Version, and improved skill in translating Hebrew and Greek finally led to demands for a new translation.

The *Revised Version* was produced by sixty-five English and Scottish scholars, including a large number of bishops. The New Testament appeared in 1881, the Old Testament in 1885, the Apocrypha in 1898, and a variant edition by American scholars, the *American Standard Version*, in 1901. Despite the advances in learning that these versions represented, their literalism and pedantic style made them unpopular. The translators were criticized as "strong in Greek, weak in English." Soon these new translations were overtaken by the rapid progress in all aspects of Biblical studies which was to make the twentieth century a golden age of Bible translations.

A New Translation of the Bible (New Testament 1913, Old Testament 1924, final revised edition of the whole 1935) is the single-handed achievement of James Moffatt, a Scottish theologian and scholar. Although Moffatt took considerable liberties with the text, often paraphrasing, sometimes correcting what he regarded as errors in the original, even rearranging sections in what he thought was the original order, it remains, according to Dr. Frederick C. Grant, one of the great translations. Though popular, even colloquial in tone, it reaches a high level of literary beauty. Its sense of reality and the clarity of its rendering of Paul's letters are noteworthy.

The Holy Scriptures According to the Massoretic Text: a New Translation, 1917 (revised 1955), was prepared by a group of American Jewish scholars headed by Max L. Margolis and published by the Jewish Publication Society. The aim of this version was "to combine the spirit of Jewish tradition with the results of biblical scholarship, ancient, medieval and modern." This Old Testament, which is widely used by Jews and often quoted by Christian scholars, is a work of sound learning. Its dignified style shows the influence of the King James Version.

A committee of scholars sponsored by the Jewish Publication Society of America is issuing a new English translation on which they have been at work for nearly twenty years. Between 1962 and 1974 they have published: The Torah, Five Megilloth, Jonah, Isaiah, Psalms, and Jeremiah. Incorporating new knowledge about the original texts and the history of the times, this projected work, when completed, will replace the 1955 version.

The Bible: An American Translation, 1931, includes Edgar J. Goodspeed's New Testament of 1923, the Old Testament of 1927 translated by J.M. Powis Smith, Alexander R. Gordon, Theophile J. Meek, and Leroy Waterman. This modern-language Bible printed in the style of a contemporary book was published by the University of Chicago Press. When Goodspeed's new translation of the Apocrypha was added, *The Complete*

Bible: An American Translation was issued in 1939. Its claim to be based on "the assured results of modern study" is largely true. When some people objected to its "journalistic" English, Goodspeed replied that the Greek New Testament itself, far from being written in polished, classical Greek, was originally set down in the common speech of first-century tradesmen and laborers.

The Holy Bible, A Translation from the Latin Vulgate in the Light of the Hebrew and Greek Originals, was completed in nine years by Ronald A. Knox, an Oxford scholar who became a convert to Catholicism. His New Testament appeared in 1945 and Old Testament in 1949. Sheed and Ward, Inc. New York published in 1956 a one-volume edition of this beautiful, readable version. Ronald Knox had already made his reputation as a mystery writer and a master of style when the Roman Catholic archbishops and bishops of England and Wales requested him to translate the Vulgate. "Latin," he explained, "is so embedded in our liturgy and in all our ecclesiastical language that a serious departure from it causes infinite confusion."

The Revised Standard Version (New Testament, 1946; Old Testament, 1952; Apocrypha, 1957) was produced by thirty-one eminent Biblical scholars from American seminaries and universities under the sponsorship of fifty denominations of the International Council of Religious Education (now part of the National Council of the Churches of Christ in the United States of America). It was initially published by Thomas Nelson and Sons, New York. This Bible is the most recent member of the Tyndale-King James-Revised Version family of English Bibles. Its translators retained as much as possible of the traditional English wording, for they aimed to preserve the language that had made the King James Bible a literary masterpiece. The Revised Standard Version is thus not an

entirely new translation. It was based on patient study of
the Hebrew and Greek texts, and includes "the best
results of modern scholarship as to the meaning of the
Scriptures." Its sense is clear; it is faithful to the original
text; and it embodies the results of modern Biblical
knowledge in a variety of fields. Consequently, many
people consider it the best and most reliable of the recent
English versions for study as well as for public and
private worship.

Three special editions of the Revised Standard Version
should be noted for their ecumenical aspects: *The Catholic Edition of the Revised Standard Version*, with essen-
tially the same text as that read by Protestants, but with
the books arranged in the Vulgate order, was published in
America by Thomas Nelson and Sons, 1965–1966. In his
forward to this edition, Richard Cardinal Cushing of
Boston stated, "Here is the message of salvation presented
now with beauty of language and clarity of expression."
The Revised Standard Version Common Bible, 1973, is
the first to be approved for use by three parts of Christen-
dom: Roman Catholic, Protestant, and Eastern Orthodox.
John Cardinal Willebrands, president of the Vatican Sec-
retariat for Christian Unity, welcomed the edition "as a
great help in the work of fulfilling the Lord's prayer that
all may be one." Moreover, Archbishop Iakovos, primate
of the Greek Orthodox Archdiocese of North and South
America, urged his people "to make full use of this new
arrangement, which uses a common text and a common
arrangement of the Holy Scripture," adding that this
Book would "greatly facilitate" Bible study with other
Christians. *The New Oxford Annotated Bible with the
Apocrypha: An Ecumenical Study Bible*, 1973, edited by
Herbert G. May and Bruce M. Metzger was published by
the Oxford University Press in a useful one-volume
edition.

The New Testament in Modern English, 1958 and the *Old Testament Prophets*, 1963, are informal translations and paraphrases by J.B. Phillips, a Church of England vicar, who began work on them in London during the blackouts of World War II. He first translated the Letters from Greek into clear, idiomatic English, often paraphrasing to make the meaning plain. His *Letters to Young Churches*, 1947, was followed by *The Gospels*, *The Young Church in Action* (Acts), and *The Book of Revelation*, all collected and issued in his one-volume New Testament. The colloquial, vigorous English of this popular translation is designed to have an impact on modern readers similar to that made on first-century Christians by the original text.

The Jerusalem Bible, 1966, was produced in England under the editorship of Father Alexander Jones of Christ's College, Liverpool, assisted by twenty-seven scholars of the Newman Association and others. It is the first complete English translation by Roman Catholics working initially from the ancient Hebrew and Greek texts rather than from the Vulgate. It is the English counterpart of *La Bible de Jérusalem*, 1961, a one-volume scholarly French version combining earlier editions and issued by the Dominican Bible School in Jerusalem under the general editorship of the late archaeologist Père Roland de Vaux, O.P. Among the men of letters who helped with the editing of the Jerusalem Bible was J.R.R. Tolkien, author of *The Lord of the Rings*. The interpretations in the Jerusalem Bible reflect *La Bible de Jérusalem*, while footnotes, introductions, historical tables, and marginal references in the English version are direct translations from the French version. Doubleday and Company, Garden City, New York, publish the American edition.

The New English Bible (New Testament, 1961; Old Testament and Apocrypha, 1970) was published by the

University Presses of both Oxford and Cambridge. This superb version is an entirely new translation from the original Hebrew and Greek texts rather than a revision of previous Bibles. It aims to "break through the barrier of familiarity" and provide the stimulus of a fresh translation for readers who tend to be "lulled rather than aroused" by time-honored phrases. It was produced under the general direction of the late Charles H. Dodd, assisted by Godfrey Driver and W.D. McHardy, all of Oxford University, and by thirty other distinguished scholars and men of letters. They were appointed in 1947 by the chief Protestant Churches of England, Scotland, Ireland, and Wales, with representatives of the Roman Catholic Church acting as observers. In their efforts to reproduce the spirit of the original and to provide a Bible "which shall be as intelligible to contemporary readers as the original version was to its first readers," the translators used the most trustworthy texts available, weighed the findings of modern scholars, and subjected their work to review by a panel of literary advisers. Because this translation is designed to convey the general effect and meaning of the original rather than to give an exact word-for-word rendering, it is perhaps less satisfactory than the more literal Revised Standard Version for certain kinds of study. One little girl remarked, "It is quite good, but it is not so holy as the old one, is it?" As a clear, fluent, accurate, and beautiful version in a living English idiom, *The New English Bible* is unsurpassed.

The New American Bible, 1970, is a fresh translation into good, ordinary English from the original languages, with critical use of all the ancient sources. It was produced by members of the Catholic Biblical Association of America assisted by four Protestant scholars. When this project was launched in 1936 under the sponsorship of the Bishops' Committee of the Confraternity of Christian

Doctrine, the aim was to make a modern English version of the Vulgate. The Confraternity New Testament was published in 1941, but two years later, in accordance with the encyclical of Pope Pius XII urging study of "the original text which . . . has more authority and greater weight than any, even the very best translation, whether ancient or modern," the Catholic Biblical Association put aside their previous work and began the present version. Though lacking the literary polish of *The New English Bible* published earlier in the same year, it is clear, readable, and faithful to the meaning of the original texts. In the spelling of proper names it follows the customary forms used in most English Bibles since the King James Version. Published by P.J. Kenedy and Sons, New York, and issued with introductions, footnotes, maps, and other aids, *The New American Bible* replaces the Douay Version and provides an excellent study Bible.

The Living Bible, 1971, published by Tyndale House, Wheaton, Illinois, and distributed by Doubleday and Company, Garden City, New York, is a paraphrase of the King James Version by Kenneth N. Taylor. He produced a clear, informal English version simple enough for his children to understand. Though controversial, it has become a phenomenal success with twenty-two million copies of some edition of the work in circulation in seven years.

Today's English Version, also known as *The Good News Bible*, was published in 1976. An edition containing the Apocrypha was issued in 1979. This version is sponsored by the American Bible Society and is in contemporary English. Instead of "word-for-word equivalence," it aims to give "meaning-for-meaning equivalence." A team of translators, under the leadership of Robert G. Bratcher of the Bible Society, produced this easily readable, free rendering. Nearly five hundred plain but sprightly line drawings by the Swiss artist Annie Vallotton illustrate the text. With its limited vocabulary, it succeeds in communicating the Bible message to young people and to readers with little formal education. More than fifty million copies of the New Testament, issued in 1966, had already been sold when the complete Bible was published.

The Holy Bible, New International Version, 1978, is published by Zondervan Corporation, Grand Rapids, Michigan, under license by the New York International Bible Society. It was produced for evangelicals by scholars who believe that the Bible is the infallible word of God. The committee of 115 men and women from more than a dozen denominations who worked for ten years on this translation aimed for "faithfulness to the original languages, beauty of style, and suitability for public and private use." They used modern language to express traditional theology. As was the case with many of the other twentieth-century Bibles listed above, the sale of this one has been phenomenal, 1.2 million copies having been bought in the four weeks following its publication.

In the twelve centuries since Caedmon's day, the English Bible, like a river augmented by many tributaries, has become a mighty force. Printing presses are now more sophisticated, scholars are better equipped to translate, and ever more people search for a Bible that meets their needs and can be read with understanding.

III
How to Read the Bible

Can one read this ancient Book today and really understand it? A new reader, opening the Bible at the beginning with a firm determination to persevere to the last page, may lose interest as early as the fifth chapter of Genesis among the genealogies of the almost incomprehensible antediluvian patriarchs. It is, of course, possible to read doggedly on through much that is dull and long-winded until you reach some well-known character or arresting verse—and happily there are many of these. But most of us do not want to read the Bible as if it were a task. It should be for us a source of increasing illumination.

According to the Book of Acts, a high official at the court of the Queen of Ethiopia was a persistent yet baffled reader. He was sitting in his chariot whiling away his journey by reading from an Isaiah scroll when Philip the evangelist encountered him on the road from Jerusalem to Gaza.

"Do you understand what you are reading?" Philip asked him. "How can I understand," replied the official, "unless someone will give me the clue?" (Acts 8.31, NEB)

Four centuries later, the great Bible translator Jerome, well aware of the difficulty of comprehending the ancient writings, declared, "You cannot make your way into the Holy Scriptures without having someone to go before you and show you the road."

The following general suggestions may help in approaching the Scriptures.

"Hear them, read, mark, learn, and inwardly digest them," advises the *Book of Common Prayer* in measured words derived from one of Francis Bacon's essays. The advice to "hear," though given at a time when Bibles were hard to obtain and not everyone could read, is pertinent today because the ear hears in many passages from the best translations a haunting music that itself suggests truths difficult to put in words.

Many seasoned Bible readers suggest that it should be approached with expectation, and read with the imagination fully involved, with a lively sense of curiosity, and above all with an alert mind that takes nothing for granted. Objectivity and the historical point of view are helpful in establishing a standard by which to evaluate whatever is read.

Anyone who reads the Bible against a broad historical background is aware that its basic message does not lie on the surface. To be sure, the sentences in our modern versions are expressed in clear and often beautiful English, but the Bible's forms of thought are ancient and many of its allusions belong to an age long past. Readers who learn to look beneath the surface of outmoded views, however, can discover the eternal message of the Bible.

The Scriptures "should be read as the utterances of real, individual men, who wrote out of their own intensely personal experience; and they should be read as the record of an historic process of discovery and revelation," wrote Charles H. Dodd in *The Authority of the Bible*.

Another dimension of Bible reading is touched upon in his *The Bible To-Day*. "Church and Bible are so closely bound together in one historical complex that it is only common sense to expect the Bible to speak to us most clearly in the context of the continuing life of the Church." "An Outline of the Faith" in the *Book of Common Prayer* of the Episcopal Church says, "We understand the meaning of the Bible by the help of the Holy Spirit, who guides the Church in the true interpretation of the Scriptures."

Finally, it appears to be almost universally true that productive Bible study is linked with prayer. As the Second Vatican Council declared, "Let them remember that prayer should accompany the reading of Sacred Scripture, so that God and man may talk together." Generations of men and women have found God through the Bible, for it has always effectively brought man and God together.

The first practical requirement for serious Bible reading is a personal copy in which passages can be freely marked, because it is necessary to blaze one's own trail through this long and admittedly complex Book. Ideally the volume chosen should be easily readable and of a comfortable size, a combination of requirements difficult to achieve in a work averaging from twelve to fifteen hundred double-column pages. One statistically minded investigator reports that it contains 1,187 chapters, 31,173 verses, and 773,692 words. Fortunately, some of the English versions are available in editions for which the publishers have achieved a combination of readable print on good paper in a book of handy size.

A careful examination of the volume's preliminaries is useful. Each word of the title-page is important and what the editors say in the Preface and Introduction should not be overlooked. Of prime importance is the Table of

Contents listing the names of the books of the Bible.
Knowledge of the order and sequence is as useful a tool to
the Bible reader as the alphabet is to one who uses a
dictionary. A little practice in looking up references and
learning the abbreviations of the various books will prove
to be time well spent. Because allusions and concepts keep
recurring in the Scriptures like themes in a symphony, the
reader needs to be able to turn easily to any verse in any
of the books in order to trace the development and
relation of ideas.

So great is the range of the Bible that it can be read from
many different points of view and readers will eventually
find their own best approach. One of the specific pro-
grams mentioned below, however, may serve as a beginning to a personally rewarding habit of regular reading.

1. Adopt one of the many available reading lists that
   cover the entire Bible and suggest a portion for each
   day of the year. The "Daily Office Lectionary" in the
   Book of Common Prayer offers selections from the
   entire Bible arranged in a two-year cycle, with the
   Psalms (with some variations) in a recurring seven-
   week cycle. If, at first, this seems too ambitious, it is
   possible to choose from the titles of "A List of Suggested Readings" which follows this chapter. This list,
   covering about one–third of the Bible, is arranged in
   historical sequence. With any course of reading it often
   proves useful to mark, date, and make notations beside
   passages that are especially illuminating.

2. Concentrate on the great stories of the Bible, especially
   those in the Gospels and Acts, and in Genesis, Exodus,
   Numbers, Joshua, 1 and 2 Samuel. The vitality and
   power of these narratives with their many layers of
   meaning may surprise one who remembers them only
   in the simplified form learned in childhood.

3. Choose one book and read it, not verse by verse, but as a whole composition in a rapid survey. It is often helpful to make one's own outline of this literary unit. Approach the book as though it were a completely new subject. Discover what is known about the author and when, where, why, and for whom he wrote. Thereafter, in slow and careful reading, note what the words actually state and try to discover what the author wanted his readers to know. Observe details. Finally, reread from the beginning, marking the verses that have particular relevance today.

4. Compare the four accounts of Jesus Christ as recorded in the Gospels. In what ways are they similar? How can their divergencies be accounted for? What unique contribution does each Gospel make to an understanding of Christ?

5. Recreate from the Bible and other sources as complete a life as possible of one Biblical character until he or she stands forth as a believable human being.

6. Record the Biblical history of one of the significant places of the Middle East, such as Jerusalem, Damascus, Jericho, Gaza, Hebron.

7. Pursue one subject through the Bible, such as: the various ways in which God became known to individuals, evidences of the tension between the idea of God's people Israel vs. God's people humankind, the position of women, justice, love, forgiveness, legal actions, occupations, journeys, dreams, cures, angels, jewels, food, music.

8. For the thought-provoking value of their unaccustomed words, buy an English translation other than your favorite one, or a French, German, or other text. It is well recognized that long familiarity with one version can sometimes lull the mind to sleep.

9. Listen to one of the records or tapes of an accomplished Bible reader. The entire King James Version has been taped on sixty-four cassettes by the actor Alexander Scourby.

From the profound depths of the Scriptures can be drawn understanding and wisdom for individual lives and for a troubled world. Kierkegaard said, "Life must be lived forward, but it can only be understood backward." In the thunders at Sinai, the exhortations of the prophets, the passionate cries of the psalmists, the gracious and living words of Jesus, the assurances of Paul, and the whole chorus of Bible voices, it is possible to hear God speaking anew to our generation.

IV
A List of Suggested Readings

The following selections contain most of the best-known stories and personalities of the Bible; some of the chief messages of the prophets; a sampling of the Book of Psalms, the other Writings, and the Apocrypha; the complete text of Luke-Acts; additional records from Matthew, Mark, and John; important excerpts from the Letters; and, finally, the rejoicings from Revelation. These readings comprise about one-third of the Bible text and include at least one passage from each book of the Old Testament and New Testament as well as a few from the Apocrypha. Except for the New Testament Letters, which are introduced in their Biblical order, the listing is arranged as far as possible in historical sequence.

THE PATRIARCHS AND THE
DAWN OF ISRAEL'S HISTORY

Genesis	1.1–2.4a	The story of creation
	2.4b–3.24	Adam and Eve live in the Garden of Eden

Genesis	4.1–16	Cain murders his brother Abel
	6.5–9.17	Noah builds the ark and survives the flood
	11.1–9	The builders of Babel are scattered abroad
	12.1–9; 15	The Lord makes a covenant with Abraham
	12.10–13.18	Abraham visits Egypt. He and Lot separate
	16; 21.8–21	The story of Hagar's son Ishmael
	18.1–15	Abraham entertains three strangers
	18.16–19.29	Sodom and Gomorrah are destroyed
	21.1–8; 22.1–19	Abraham prepares to sacrifice Isaac
	23	Abraham purchases a grave for Sarah
	24	Isaac marries Rebekah
	25.19–34; 27	Jacob cheats his brother Esau
	27.46–28.22	Jacob has a dream at Bethel
	29.1–30	The romance of Jacob and Rachel
	32–33	Jacob returns to the Promised Land
	37	Joseph's brothers sell him into slavery

Genesis	39	Joseph becomes Potiphar's chief official
	40–41	Joseph rises to power in Egypt
	42.1–45.15	Joseph's brothers go to Egypt
	45.16–46.7	Jacob and his sons move to Egypt
Exodus	1.1–2.10	Moses' mother hides him in a basket
	2.11–22	Moses flees from Egypt
	3.1–4.17	A voice speaks to Moses from the burning bush
	4.27–5.23	Pharaoh lays heavier burdens on Israelites
	7.8–24	The first of the ten plagues
	12.1–50	The Israelites leave Egypt
	13.20–14.20	Pharaoh pursues the fleeing Israelites
	14.21–30	The Lord saves Israel at the sea
	15.1–21	The people sing a song of faith and victory

ISRAEL BECOMES THE PEOPLE OF GOD

Exodus	15.22–17.16	In the wilderness the people suffer from thirst, hunger, and enemy attacks
	19.1–20.21	Moses receives the Covenant and the Ten Commandments at Sinai

Exodus 32		The people worship a golden calf
	34	The Lord renews his covenant with Israel
Leviticus 19		"You shall be holy; for I the Lord your God am holy"
Numbers	13.1–14.12	Twelve spies survey the land of Canaan
	17.1–11	Aaron's rod buds and bears fruit
	20.1–13	Moses strikes water from the rock
	22–24	Balaam blesses the Israelites
	27.1–11	Five sisters establish the right of women to inherit
Deuteronomy 6		The meaning of the first commandment
	7.6–11	"A people holy to the Lord"
	22.1–8; 24.10–22; 25.13–16	Laws protecting the rights and welfare of others
	32.45–52; 34	The death of Moses
Joshua	2	Joshua sends spies into Jericho
	3–4	Israel crosses the Jordan on dry ground
	6	Jericho is besieged and captured

Joshua	9	The Gibeonites deceive the Is- raelites
	10.1–27	Joshua subdues southern Palestine
	24	The Israelites renew the Covenant at Shechem
	2.6–23	"Then the Lord raised up judges"
	4–5	Deborah and Barak lead Israel to victory
	6–8	Gideon saves Israel and re- fuses the kingship
	11.29–40	Jephthah makes a rash vow
	13.1–16.31	Samson's story
Ruth	1–4	The story of Ruth, Naomi, and Boaz

ISRAEL'S FIRST KINGS

1 Samuel	1.1–2.20	Samuel's birth; his dedication to the Lord
	3	The Lord calls Samuel
	4	The Philistines capture the ark; the old priest Eli dies
	9–10	Samuel annoints Saul; the people acclaim him king
	15	Samuel rejects Saul for his disobedience
	16	David is anointed by Samuel; plays the lyre for Saul

1 Samuel	17	David defeats Goliath
	18.1–19.18	David flees from Saul's court
	24	Saul's life is spared by David
	25	Abigail becomes David's wife
	28.3–25	Saul consults the woman of Endor
	31	Saul and his sons die in battle
2 Samuel	1	David learns of Saul's death and mourns for him
	2.1–11; 5.1–12	David becomes king of Judah and Israel
1 Chronicles	11.4–19	David conquers Jerusalem; receives water from the well in Bethlehem
2 Samuel	6	The Ark is brought into Jerusalem
	9	David shows kindness to Jonathan's son
	11–12.15	David marries Bathsheba; is denounced by Nathan the prophet
	12.15–25	The death of David's son
	15.1–23; 18	Absalom revolts against his father
	24	David builds an altar on Araunah's threshing floor
1 Chronicles	28–29	David's instructions concerning the Temple and the accession of Solomon

THE GREAT PROPHETS AND THEIR TIMES

2 Kings	9.1–13	Jehu is anointed king of Israel
	9.14–10.11	Jehu massacres the royal family of Ahab
Amos	1–2	"Thus says the Lord"
	3–5	"Let justice roll down like waters, / and righteousness like an ever-flowing stream"
	6	"Woe to those who are at ease in Zion"
	7.10–17	Amos confronts Amaziah at Bethel
Hosea	11.1–9	"When Israel was a child, I loved him"
	14	"Return, O Israel, to the Lord your God"
2 Kings	11	Young Joash is proclaimed king of Judah
2 Chronicles	26	The reign of King Uzziah
Isaiah	6	Isaiah is called to prophesy
	1.1–2.4	"Hear, O heavens, . . . for the Lord has spoken"
	5	The allegory of the vineyard; Isaiah's six reproaches
	9.1–7; 11.1–9	"The people who walked in darkness / have seen a great light"
Micah	4.1–7; 5.2–4	Micah's vision of peace and of the coming shepherd king of Israel from Bethlehem

Micah	6.6–8	"What does the Lord require of you?"
Zephaniah	1.14–18	"The great day of the Lord is near"
Jeremiah	1	Jeremiah is called to prophesy
	2.1–19	"They have forsaken me, / the fountain of living waters"
2 Kings	22.1–23.3	The book of the Law is found in the Temple
Nahum	1.12–3.19	An ode celebrating the fall of hated Nineveh
Habakkuk	1.2–2.4	Habakkuk ponders the problem of evil
Jeremiah	31.27–34	"Behold . . . I will make a new covenant with the house of Israel"
	32.1–15	Jeremiah buys an ancestral field as a sign of his confidence in the Lord
	37–38	The story of the prophet's imprisonment and rescue

THE EXILE AND THE RETURN

2 Kings	25.1–21; Psalm 137	Jerusalem is captured; the Babylonian exile begins
Lamentations	1	Lament over a destroyed city
Obadiah	1–14	Obadiah's bitter indictment of Edom

Ezekiel	1–3	Ezekiel's vision of the divine chariot; his commission as a prophet
	18	"I will judge you . . . every one according to his ways"
	37.1–14	The Vision of the Valley of Dry Bones
	40.1–16; 43.1–9	From Ezekiel's vision of the new Temple
Isaiah	40.1–11	Second Isaiah promises the restoration of Israel
	40.12–41.4	God the Creator and Lord of history
	41.8–13; 42.1–9; 49.1–6	From the "servant psalms" of Second Isaiah
	43.1–44.8	"Fear not, for I have redeemed you"
	49.8–26	"Sing for joy, O heavens"
	51.1–16	"Look to the rock from which you were hewn"
	52	"Put on your beautiful garments, / O Jerusalem"
	53	"Surely he has borne our griefs"
	55	"Ho, every one who thirsts, / come to the waters"
	60	"Arise, shine; for your light has come"
	61	"The Spirit of the Lord God is upon me"

Isaiah	65.17–25	"For behold, I create new heavens and a new earth"
Haggai	1.1–2.9	Haggai summons the people to rebuild the Temple
Zechariah	1–6	Zechariah's visions
Ezra	5.1–5; 6.13–22	The building of the second Temple
Nehemiah	1–2	Nehemiah goes to Jerusalem
	4; 6.15–16	Jerusalem's walls are rebuilt
	8	Ezra reads the Law to the people
	9	The people renew the Covenant
Joel	1.1–2.27	A locust plague and drought provoke a call to repentance
	2.28–3.17	"I will pour out my spirit on all flesh"
Malachi	1.6–3.5	"Behold, I send my messenger to prepare the way before me"
Jonah	1–4	The story of a reluctant prophet
Esther	1–8	Esther saves her people

POETRY AND PROSE OF THE OLD TESTAMENT

Job	1–3	Job suffers dire affliction
	4–5	Eliphaz asks, "Who that was innocent ever perished?"

Job	9–10	Job questions God's ways
	19	"I know that my Redeemer lives."
	28	A soliloquy on wisdom
	31	Job's moral code
	38.1–42.6	"Then the Lord answered Job out of the whirlwind"
	42	Job's answer to the Lord
Psalms	1; 8; 9	"Blessed is the man"; "O Lord . . . how majestic is thy name in all the earth"; "The Lord sits enthroned for ever"
	15; 16	"O Lord . . . who shall dwell on thy holy hill"; "I have a goodly heritage"
	19; 22; 23	"The heavens are telling the glory of God"; "My God, my God, why has thou forsaken me"; "The Lord is my shepherd"
	24; 27; 29	"The earth is the Lord's"; "The Lord is my light"; "The voice of the Lord is upon the waters"
	34; 42; 46	"I sought the Lord, and he answered me"; "My soul thirsts for God"; "God is our refuge and strength"
	50; 51	"Offer to God a sacrifice of thanksgiving"; "Create in me a clean heart, O God"

Psalms	63; 65; 84	"Thy steadfast love is better than life"; "Thou crownest the year with thy bounty"; "How lovely is thy dwelling place"
	90; 91; 92	"Lord, thou hast been our dwelling place"; "He who dwells in the shelter of the Most High"; "It is good to give thanks to the Lord"
	95; 100; 103	"O come, let us sing to the Lord"; "We are his people"; "Bless the Lord, O my soul"
	104	"O Lord, how manifold are thy works!"
	113; 121; 122	"From the rising of the sun to its setting"; "I lift up my eyes to the hills"; "I was glad when they said to me"
	130; 133; 139	"Out of the depths I cry to thee, O Lord"; "When brothers dwell in unity"; "O Lord, thou has searched me and known me!"
	145; 148; 150	"The Lord is gracious and merciful"; Praise from the whole creation; "Let everything that breathes praise the Lord!"
Proverbs	3	Advice to a young man
	6.6–19; 10–11; 15	Wise counsels

Proverbs 31.10–31	An ideal wife
Ecclesiastes 1–3	On the futility of life
11.7–12.8	Thoughts on old age
Song of Solomon 2, 4	Love Songs
Daniel 3	The three young men are saved from the fiery furnace
5	Handwriting appears on the wall at Belshazzar's feast
6	Daniel is delivered in the lions' den
7	The apocalyptic vision of four beasts

THE APOCRYPHA

Wisdom 2.23–3.9	"But God created man for immortality' (NEB)
6.1–25	"The true beginning of wisdom is the desire to learn" (NEB)
Ecclesiasticus (Sirach) 28.13–26	"Curses on the gossip and the tale-bearer!" (NEB)
38.1–14	"Healing comes from the Most High"
44.1–15	"Let us now praise famous men"
Baruch 4.21–5.9	"Take courage, my children"
Song of the Three vv. 29–34	"Blessed art thou, O Lord, God of our Fathers"

Song of the Three
> vv. 35–65   "Bless the Lord, all works of the Lord"

THE GOSPEL ACCORDING TO LUKE

Luke	1.1–25, 57–80	Foreword. The birth of John the Baptist
	1.26–56	The angel Gabriel foretells the birth of Jesus
	2	Jesus is born in Bethlehem; is presented in the Temple; visits Jerusalem during his boyhood
	3.1–4.13	Jesus is baptized by John; is tempted in the wilderness
	4.14–44	Jesus begins his ministry in Galilee; is rejected at Nazareth; preaches and heals in Capernaum
	5.1–6.16	He calls his disciples; heals the sick; encounters opposition
	6.17–49	His Sermon on the Plain
	7.1–8.3	He heals a centurion's servant; raises a widow's son; commends John the Baptist; is anointed by a sinful woman
	8.4–25	He tells the parable of the sower; speaks of his true family; stills a storm;

Luke	8.26–56	Heals a demoniac; raises Jairus's daughter; heals a suffering woman
	9.1–17	Twelve disciples are sent forth; a multitude is fed
	9.18–50	Peter confesses his faith; Jesus is transfigured; he heals an epileptic; teaches about true greatness
	9.51–10.24	Jesus sets "his face to go to Jerusalem"; is rejected by a Samaritan village; teaches about discipleship; sends forth seventy disciples
	10.25–11.13	He tells the story of the Good Samaritan; visits Martha and Mary; instructs his disciples about prayer
	11.14–12.12	He answers his critics; warns against Pharisaism
	12.13–13.9	He teaches about false security and the coming of God's kingdom
	13.10–14.6	He heals on the Sabbath; teaches about the kingdom; laments over Jerusalem
	14.7–16.31	A collection of his parables and other teachings
	17	He instructs his disciples; heals ten lepers; speaks of the coming kingdom

Luke	18.1–14; 19.11–27	Three parables
	18.15–19.10	Jesus blesses the children; instructs the rich young ruler; heals a blind beggar; visits Zacchaeus
	19.28–46	Jesus enters Jerusalem; cleanses the Temple
	19.47–20.18	He answers the priests and scribes; tells the parable of the tenants of a vineyard
	20.19–47	His opponents try to entrap him in questions
	21	He comments on the poor widow's offering; foretells the future
	22.1–6	Judas plots with the priests and scribes
	22.7–38	The last supper of Jesus and his disciples
	22.39–65	He goes to Gethsemane; is betrayed and arrested; Peter denies him
	22.66–23.25	Jesus is tried by the Sanhedrin and sentenced to death by Pontius Pilate
	23.26–56	The crucifixion and burial of Jesus
	24.1–11	The women and Peter find his tomb empty

| **Luke** | 24.12–53 | The risen Christ appears on the Emmaus road and in Jerusalem |

EVENTS AND TEACHINGS FROM THE GOSPELS OF MATTHEW, MARK, AND JOHN

Matthew	1.18–2.23	Stories of Jesus' birth; the visit of the wise men; the flight into Egypt
John	1.1–18	"The Word became flesh and dwelt among us"
	1.19–34	John the Baptist bears witness to Jesus
	1.35–51	Peter and Andrew, Philip and Nathanael become disciples
	2.1–12	Jesus and his mother attend a wedding in Cana
	3.1–21	Nicodemus the Pharisee visits Jesus
	4.1–43	In Samaria Jesus talks to a woman at the well
	4.46–5.18	Jesus heals the official's son and a lame man
	5.19–47	Jesus explains his Sonship
Matthew	5–7	His Sermon on the Mount
Mark	4.1–34	He teaches in parables
Matthew	14.22–33	He walks on the sea

John	9	He heals a man born blind
	10	Jesus as the Good Shepherd
Mark	10.35–45	James and John seek honors for themselves
John	11	Jesus raises Lazarus from death
	12.20–50	Certain Greeks seek Jesus; many of his own people do not believe in him
	13.1–30	Events at the last supper
	13.31–16.33	Farewell discourses of Jesus
	17	Jesus' high-priestly prayer
Matthew	27–28	Matthew's account of Jesus' death and resurrection
Mark	14–16	Mark's account of Jesus' death and the empty tomb
John	20	The risen Christ appears to Mary Magdalene and to his disciples
	21	He appears to seven disciples at the sea

THE ACTS OF THE APOSTLES

| **Acts** | 1 | Preface; Christ's ascension; his waiting followers; the choice of Matthias |
| | 2.1–36 | The Holy Spirit is given to the Church; Peter preaches |

Acts	15.1–35	The council of Jerusalem admits Gentiles to the Church
	15.36–16.10	On Paul's second journey he crosses Asia Minor
	16.11–40	Paul sails to Macedonia and enters Philippi
	17	Paul visits Thessalonica, Beroea, and Athens
	18.1–22	At Corinth Paul meets Aquila and Priscilla
	18.23–19.41	On his third missionary journey Paul remains two years in Ephesus
	20.1–21.14	After visits in Macedonia and Achaia, Greece, Paul returns, via Ephesus and Caesarea, to Jerusalem
	21.15–40	Paul is rescued from a Temple mob
	22.1–29	Paul speaks in his own defense
	22.30–23.11	Paul's case produces dissension in the Sanhedrin
	23.12–35	Roman authorities send Paul to Caesarea to save him from a Jewish plot
	24	Felix, the governor, keeps Paul in prison
	25.1–22	Paul appeals his case to Rome
	25.23–26.32	King Agrippa and his wife listen to Paul

2 Corinthians	4	Paul discourses on his ministry
	5.1–6.10	"If any one is in Christ, he is a new creation"
	7	Paul's joy in his good relations with the church at Corinth
	9	An appeal for contributions for the poor in Jerusalem
	11.16–12.13	Paul describes his life as an apostle
Galatians	1–2	Paul defends his apostolic authority
	3.1–4.7	"In Christ Jesus you are all sons of God, through faith"
	5	Christ has set us free that we might remain a free people
	6	Counsels and a personal benediction
Ephesians	1	"He destined us in love to be his sons through Jesus Christ"
	2	"The household of God"
	3	"The unsearchable riches of Christ"
	4	"One Lord, one faith, one baptism, one God and Father of us all"
	5.1–20	"Walk in love, as Christ loved us"

Ephesians	5.21–6.24	Relationships in the Christian family
Philippians	1.1–26	"For me to live is Christ"
	1.27–2.18	"Let your manner of life be worthy of the gospel of Christ"
	3	"Our commonwealth is in heaven"
	4	"Rejoice in the Lord always"
Colossians	1.3–23	"In him [Christ] all the fulness of God was pleased to dwell"
	1.24–2.23	"You have come to fulness of life in him"
	3.1–4.6	How to live a Christian life
1 Thessalonians	4–5	"You learned from us how you ought to live and to please God"
2 Thessalonians	2.13–3.18	"Brethren, stand firm"

ADDITIONAL LETTERS AND WRITINGS BY PAUL AND OTHERS

1 Timothy	2–3	Instructions concerning church organization and the Christian life
	4	"Train yourself in godliness"
	5–6	The duties of a pastor
2 Timothy	2.1–4.5	The pastor and his flock
	4.6–22	Paul's farewell

Titus	2.1–3.11	Sound doctrine and Christian living
Philemon		Paul's plea to the owner of a runaway slave
Hebrews	1–2	Christ as the final spokesman of God
	4.14–5.11	Christ our high priest
	11	"Now faith is the assurance of things hoped for"
	12	"Since we are surrounded by so great a cloud of witnesses"
	13	"Let brotherly love continue"
James	1–2	"Be doers of the word, and not hearers only"
	3	On controlling the tongue
	5.13–20	Spiritual healing and the power of prayer
1 Peter	1	"Born anew to a living hope"
	2.1–10	The holy priesthood of believers
	5	"Cast all your anxieties on him, for he cares about you"
2 Peter	1	The Scriptures came from "men moved by the Holy Spirit"
	3.8–18	"We wait for new heavens and a new earth in which righteousness dwells"

1 John	1	"That which we have seen and heard we proclaim also to you"
	2	"He who loves his brother abides in the light"
	3	"Beloved, we are God's children now"
	4	"God is love"
	5	"This is the victory that overcomes the world, our faith"
2 John; 3 John		Personal letters from the "elder"
Jude		Fortify yourselves against heretics; doxology
Revelation	1	John's salutation; his vision of Christ in glory
	2–3	Letters to the seven churches of Asia
	4	The throne in heaven
	5	Vision of the Lamb
	6	When the seals are opened the four horsemen appear
	7.9–17	The multitude of saints stand before the throne of the Lamb
	11.15–19	"The kingdom of the world has become the kingdom of our Lord and of his Christ"

Revelation	14.1–7, 12–16	"Lo, on Mount Zion stood the Lamb"
	18	An apocalyptic prophecy of "Babylon's" doom
	19.1–16	"The Lord our God the Almighty reigns"
	21.1–22.5	"Behold, the dwelling of God is with men"
	22.6–21	"Come, Lord Jesus!"

V

The Divine Names

THE SIGNIFICANCE OF A NAME
IN BIBLICAL TIMES

A person's name was more than a convenient label to the ancient Hebrews. They believed that, in addition to distinguishing one individual from another, a name somehow contained the essence of personality and provided the key to a man's or a woman's character. "As his name is, so is he" (1 Sam 25.25). A dramatic change in a person's life sometimes resulted in a new name, as when Jacob's name was changed to Israel (Gen 35.10). To the question, "What's in a name?" the Hebrews would have replied, "The very kernel of being." Moreover, he who pronounces the name gains a mysterious power to influence and control whoever is named.

The Hebrews thought that it was essential to know God's name, and in times of distress they habitually "called on the name of the Lord" (Ps 116.4). Sometimes the Bible mentions God's name virtually as a substitute for God himself (Deut 12.11). When the priests were instructed to convey the Lord's power to his people, they were told to "put my name upon the people of Israel"

(Num 6.27). Moses' urgent desire to know the name of the deity who spoke to him from the burning bush perhaps indicated his purpose to gain access to divine power through invoking the Name. The mysterious name revealed to him was *Yahweh*, meaning "I AM WHO I AM" or "I will be what I will be" (Ex 3.13–15). Though this name did not explain or define God's character, it suggested a Being of unlimited existence.

A central idea running through the Bible is that God's name is itself holy. This idea, probably a development of the primitive notion that a name could be used to exert magical control, underlies the Third Commandment (Ex 20.7), which prohibits the misuse of the Lord's name. False swearing (Lev 19.12), reviling God (Ex 22.28), and blaspheming the Name (Lev 24.11–16) were all prohibited, the latter being subject to death by stoning.

The importance of God's name to the Hebrews is attested by many passages in the Bible. People sought personal access to the Lord by invoking his name (Ps 54.1; Zech 13.9). They derived comfort from the divine assurance, "I will protect him because he knows my name" (Ps 91.14). Oaths taken in God's name were binding (Deut 6.13). Prophetic words spoken or written in the name of God were believed to have divine authority (Dan 9.6). This conviction impelled three officials of Jehoiakim's court to protest the king's impiety in burning the scroll of Jeremiah's prophecies (Jer 36.20–25).

In the invocation of the Lord's Prayer (Mt. 6.9; Lk 11.2), Jesus taught his disciples to pray to their Father in heaven, "Hallowed be thy name." At the end of his ministry, after Jesus had revealed to his followers the nature and purpose of God so that they might be included in the divine love, he prayed "I made known to them thy name" (Jn 17.26).

Note: The names listed below, except for *Dominus*, are from the original text of the Bible and from its principal English versions.

THE NAMES OF GOD

Abba   The Aramaic for "father." It was a distinctive and intimate term used by Jesus in prayer (Mk 14.36), and appropriated by the Church for the liturgy (Rom 8.15). It is preserved in three places in the New Testament, the two references above and Galatians 4.6. *See* Father.

Adonai   The Hebrew word used as a substitute for the ineffable name *Yahweh*. It means "my Lord" and in copies of the Scriptures it was written above the four consonants of the divine name because it was to be pronounced instead of Yahweh. *Adonijah*, meaning "Jah (or Yah) is Lord," though actually a statement of faith, was the name David gave to his fourth son (2 Sam 3.4). *See* Jehovah.

Almighty, The   The English translation of the Hebrew *Shaddai* (Ps 91.1). In the Revised Standard Version "the Almighty" occurs fifty-eight times (more than half of which are found in Job). Sometimes it appears in the form of "God Almighty" or "the Lord God the Almighty." *See* Shaddai.

Dominus   The Latin for "Lord" and "God" and the equivalent of the Hebrew *Adonai* and the Greek *Kyrios*. It does not appear in English Bibles.

El   A general Semitic word for a god. Probably its root meaning is "power." According to the ancient literature found at Ras Shamra, the supreme god of the

Canaanite pantheon was El. In the Hebrew text of the Old Testament *El* is sometimes used poetically for the God of Israel, but English Bibles translate this name usually as "God." *El* appears in such compound proper names as: Isra-el, Beth-el, Eli-jah, Ezeki-el. *See also* Eli

Eli   The Hebrew and, also, Aramaic form of *El*. On the cross, Jesus, quoting Psalm 22.1, called on God by this name (Mt 27.46; cf. Mk 15.34). *See also* Eloi.

Elohim   The usual Hebrew word for "gods." The name, being plural, may reflect an ancient polytheism, but in the Bible this plural is used as an intensive and conveys the idea that the being of all gods is concentrated in the God of Israel. It is translated "God" in English Bibles. Despite the suggestion of a heavenly council of gods in the passage, "Then God [Elohim] said, 'Let us make man in our image. . .' " (Gen 1.26), the Hebrew writer clearly used the so-called plural of majesty to emphasize Israel's monotheistic faith in God as the sum total of deity.

Eloi   A variation of *Eli* (Mk 15.34).

Elyon   A divine title used by the Canaanites to mean "Most High." *El Elyon*, translated "God Most High," was the name of Melchizedek's God, who is identified with the God of Israel (Gen 14.18–23). *See also* Most High.

Eternal, The   A rendering of *Yahweh* introduced by French scholars and used by James Moffatt in his translation of the Bible in an effort to avoid the archaic and racial overtones of the name the ancient Hebrews gave their God. *See* Yahweh.

Father   A title for God reflecting Israel's reliance on his care, compassion, forgiveness, and love. Though this concept appears throughout the Old Testament (Ex 4.22;

Ps 103.13, etc.), the title itself is used there only a few times (Ps 89.26; Isa 63.16; Jer 3.19; etc.). In the Gospels, however, it occurs seventy-five times, most frequently in Matthew and John, though it appears in every New Testament book except 3 John. This repeated use reflects the emphasis Jesus placed upon the Fatherhood of God, a Fatherhood that, according to his teachings, includes everyone, whether good or evil, Jew or Gentile. The Aramaic *Abba* "Father", that Jesus used in prayer, has been preserved in many translations. *See* Abba.

God   A pre-Christian word from the Germanic family of languages used to translate Hebrew and Greek names for the Supreme Being. The word appears singly or in combination 4,257 times in the Revised Standard Version.

"I AM WHO I AM"   The usual interpretation given in Exodus 3.14 of the meaning of God's personal name. *See* Yahweh.

Jehovah   A hybrid name combining the consonants of the sacred name *Yahweh* with the vowels of *Adonai.* The consonants were Y H W H (or J H V H), as written in the consonantal Hebrew script. This mixed name, which was invented in the sixteenth century, was an attempt to pronounce God's personal name whose original sound, after centuries of disuse, had been forgotten. Though Tyndale introduced *Jehovah* into the first printed English Bible, the King James Version used it only four times (Ex 6.3; Ps 83.18; Isa 12.2; 26.4), replacing it elsewhere with the capitalized "LORD." *Jehovah*, however, was featured in the Revised Version, 1881–1885, and in the American Standard Version, 1901, thus becoming for many people their preferred name for God. But the Revised Standard Version, 1946–1952, as its preface explains, returned to the style of the King James Version by using "LORD" instead of *Jehovah.*

Kyrios   The Greek for "Lord." It was the word used in the Septuagint for the Hebrew *Yahweh.* This name does not appear in English Bibles. *Kyrie eleison,* meaning "Lord, have mercy," is used liturgically.

LORD   An English word adopted to represent the Hebrew Y H W H (Yahweh). It is the equivalent of the Greek *Adonai,* which the Jews in the Greek period substituted for the ineffable name, *Yahweh.* In the King James, the Revised Standard, and other versions, LORD printed in capital letters is used wherever *Yahweh* appears in the original Hebrew text. When Jesus Christ is designated as Lord, only the first letter of the name is capitalized. Alone, or in combination with "God" or other divine appellations, LORD and Lord occur some 7,700 times in the Revised Standard Version.

Most High   The translation of *Elyon* and a name for the LORD. It is used fifty-three times in the Old Testament (Deut 32.8; Ps 9.2, etc.) *See* Elyon.

Shaddai   The Hebrew name of God used by the patriarchs Abraham, Isaac, and Jacob (Gen 17.1; 48.3; Ex 6.3). *El Shaddai* may have meant "God, the One of the Mountains." The Greek Bible sometimes rendered this name *Pantocrator* "Almighty". *See* Almighty, The.

Yah   A shortened form of God's personal name, Yahweh.

Yahweh   A modern reconstruction of the ancient name of the God of Israel. It is derived from the Tetragrammaton, the four consonants Y H W H which comprised the name of God as written in the consonantal Hebrew script. Awe and superstitious fear of profaning the divine name eventually caused the Hebrews to avoid uttering Y H W H. In the ensuing centuries, because their alphabet lacked vowels to indicate pronunciation, the original sound of God's name became lost. *See* Jehovah. From a study of the early Church fathers, modern scholars believe that Yahweh is approximately the original pronunciation of this name. Yahweh is used in the Jerusalem Bible, but it does not appear in the Revised Standard Version, LORD being printed wherever Y H W H appears in the Hebrew text. *See* LORD.

At Mt. Sinai (or Horeb) it was revealed to Moses that *Yahweh* was the personal name of the God who spoke to him from the burning bush (Ex 3.14) and that this was the same God whom the patriarchs had worshiped under another name (Ex 6.2–3).

As the being and character of God does not seem to be revealed in the cryptic translation of his name, "I AM WHO I AM," this appellation perhaps implied a rebuke to those ancient Israelites who believed in the magic potency of a divine name. If they indeed desired to know God's true name in order to command his presence and appropriate his power, this name gave them no encouragement. Moreover, "I AM WHO I AM," indicates the impossibility of adequately defining God or of including his transcendent being in a name.

Though the meaning of the name is obscure, scholars trace its derivation to an archaic root of the verb "to be" and interpret its basic meaning variously as "He who is"; "He is present, ready to help"; "He who speaks"; "He who brings into being whatever comes into being."

Whatever the origin and literal meaning of *Yahweh*, it acquired a wealth of concrete meaning for the people of Israel. They knew him as "the LORD your God, who brought you out of the land of Egypt, out of the house of bondage" (Ex 20.2). Moses learned of Yahweh's graciousness and mercy toward his people (Ex 33.18–19). Throughout their history, the mighty acts of Yahweh added fresh concepts to the meaning of his name. Perhaps the Biblical idea of Yahweh is best expressed in the word *living*, which is used with the divine names more than thirty-three times in the Bible (Deut 5.26; Ps 42.2; Jn 6.57; etc.).

Yahweh of Sabaoth   A Hebrew name expressing the sovereign might and majesty of God. In most English versions it is translated "LORD of hosts." Originally it referred to the Lord, the protector of his people in this role of commanding the armies of Israel. Later its meaning included the idea of God as sovereign over the "hosts of heaven" and all the cosmic forces. This name appears in the Old Testament nearly three hundred times, most frequently in the prophets (Isa 51.15; Jer 10.16; Amos 5.27; etc.). David used it in his defiance of Goliath (1 Sam 17.45), and in Psalm 24 it figures in the final response.

Other Designations:
>   Alpha and Omega, Rev 1.8
>   Ancient of Days, Dan 7.13,22
>   Creator, Eccles 12.1; Isa 40.28
>   Holy One of Israel, The, Ps 71.22; Isa 1.4
>   Judge, Gen 18.25
>   King, Ps 44.4.; Mal 1.14; Zech 14.16
>   King of Glory, Ps 24.7
>   Redeemer, Isa 43.14; Ps 19.14; Jer 50.34
>   Rock, Deut 32.4; Ps 89.26
>   Savior, Ps 106.21; Isa 43.3
>   Shepherd, Ps 23.1; 80.1

THE NAMES AND TITLES OF JESUS CHRIST

Christ   The title given to Jesus of Nazareth as the Messiah. It is derived from the Hebrew *mashiah* "anointed one", whose Greek translation is *Christos*. The recognition of Jesus as the Messiah of Hebrew prophecy, the Christ, is the central theme of the Gospel of Mark, a theme that reaches a climax in Peter's declaration, "You are the Christ" (Mk 8.29). Though actually a title, *Christ* alone or combined with *Jesus* soon became a proper name. It appears in the New Testament some five hundred times. *See also* Messiah.

Jesus   The personal name of him whose title is Christ. It is derived from the Hebrew *Joshua*, "Yahweh is salvation," which is translated *Jesous* in Greek. Both *Joshua* and *Jesus* mean "Savior," as is made clear in the angel's words to Joseph, "you shall call his name Jesus, for he will save his people from their sins" (Mt 1.21). Because the name was a common one among first-century Jews (Col. 4.11), Jesus was distinguished from others of the same name by such descriptive phrases as : "Jesus of Nazareth" (Lk 24.19); "Jesus, Son of David" (Mk 10.47); "the Nazarene, Jesus" (Mk 14.67); "the prophet Jesus" (Mt 21.11); "Jesus Christ our Lord" (Rom 1.4). The name occurs more than nine hundred times in the New Testament. The symbol, or monogram, IHS is a contraction of the name Jesus in Greek.

King of the Jews   An appellation given by the Wise Men of the infancy story (Mt 2.2). Jesus, however, did not claim this messianic title, nor did his disciples use it except in Philip's exclamation, "You are the King of Israel" (Jn 1.49) and in the crowd's shout, "Blessed is the King who comes in the name of the Lord" (Lk 19.38). Pilate's question, "Are you the King of the Jews?" (Mk 15.2), was the chief issue at Jesus' Roman trial where, according to John's Gospel, Jesus replied, "My kingship is not of this world" (Jn 18.36). Nevertheless, he was mocked and taunted with the title and Pilate had it inscribed above the cross.

Kyrios   A Greek title translated "Lord" in the English Bible.

Logos   A Greek term used in the prologue of the Gospel of John to refer to Christ. It is translated "the Word" in English Bibles. Christian theologians used *Logos* to designate the second person of the Trinity. *See* Word, The.

Lord   The title given to Jesus by the early Church to express their primary faith in him as Lord of the Church, one to whom allegiance and devotion is due (Acts 2.36). *See above*, The Names of God, LORD. The English word is derived from an Anglo-Saxon word meaning "loaf keeper," which designated the master of a large estate. "Lord" became the translation of the Greek *Kyrios* that appears in the original text of the New Testament. The title, used frequently after the resurrection, is found about four hundred times in Acts, the Letters, and Revelation. "Jesus is Lord" (1 Cor 12.3; cf. Acts 16.31) was probably the earliest Christian creed. Paul, who quotes an early Aramaic prayer to Jesus, *Marana tha*, "Our Lord come!" (1 Cor 16.22; cf. Rev 22.20), generally refers to him as "the Lord Jesus Christ" (Rom 1.7).

When the word occurs in the Synoptic Gospels, it is usually, like the modern *sir*, a polite form of address to a teacher or rabbi as, "Lord, teach us to pray" (Lk 11.1). But sometimes it is a later theological comment reflecting faith in the Lordship of Jesus, as in the statement, "a Savior who is Christ the Lord" (Lk 2.11).

Master   A title for Jesus used seventeen times in the Revised Standard Version of the Gospels and Letters. It is the translation of several Greek words meaning "teacher" or a person in authority (Mt 26.25; Mk 10.51). *See also* Rabbi, Teacher.

Messiah   The English form of the Hebrew *mashiah* "anointed", translated into Greek as *Christos.* In only two places (Jn 1.41; 4.25) does the New Testament apply this title to Jesus. Originally *mashiah* referred to anointed kings and high priests of Israel (1 Sam 24.6), but later it became the designation of the future ideal king who was expected to deliver the Jews from their enemies and restore the kingdom to Israel. Because the title had political overtones and would have compelled people's blind allegiance rather than awaken their understanding and willing trust, Jesus seems to have avoided calling himself the Messiah. When John the Baptist asked if Jesus were the Messiah, Jesus did not explicitly claim Messianic authority, but pointed to his acts, which were those of the expected Messiah. (Mt 11.2–5; cf. Isa 29.18–19; 35.5–6; 61.1). When Peter asserted, "You are the Christ," Jesus "strictly charged the disciples to tell no one that he was the Christ" (Mt 16.16, 20). Though the full meaning that Jesus attached to the role of Messiah is not known, it seems clear that he believed it to include the idea of the Suffering Servant mentioned by Isaiah (Isa 53.4–6; Mk 8.31). *See also* Christ.

Rabbi   A Hebrew word meaning "my master." It is found only in the Gospel of John where, in the Revised Standard Version, it is used eight times by the disciples and others as a title of respect for Jesus (Jn 1.38, etc.). *See also* Master, Teacher.

Rabboni   The Aramaic form of *rabbi.* Its only occurrence in the Revised Standard Version is in Mary Magdalene's exclamation upon recognizing the risen Christ (Jn 20.16).

Savior   The title expressing the New Testament's basic message that Jesus Christ brings salvation to mankind. Surprisingly, the apostolic Church seldom used this appellation. It is applied to Jesus only twice in the Gospels (Lk 2.11; Jn 4.42), twice in Acts (Acts 5.31; 13.23), and twice in Paul's Letters (Eph 5.23; Phil 3.20). But in the later writings of the Church and in the Pastoral Letters, it is found no fewer than ten times (2 Tim 1.10; Tit 1.4; 2 Pet 1.1; etc.). This may possibly be explained by the fact that during the apostolic period the Roman emperors were called "saviors." A later generation of Christians, however, boldly protested emperor-worship by declaring, "Not Caesar but Christ is the true Savior."

The Old Testament, notably in Isaiah, gives this title to God (Isa 45.15), as does the New Testament in eight instances (Lk 1.47; 1 Tim 2.3; etc.).

Son of David   A phrase expressing the Jewish conviction that the future Messiah would spring from the royal line of David. The genealogies in Matthew and Luke mention David as an ancestor of Jesus (Mt 1.6; Lk 3.31). Though anyone claiming descent from David could be addressed by this title, its use by many who sought to be cured by Jesus indicates their belief in his qualification for Messiahship (Mk 10.47).

Son of God   A title accorded to Jesus about one hundred times in the New Testament to express the faith of the early Church in the uniqueness of his person. Whether or not Jesus used this title is uncertain, though, when asked, he did not deny it at his trial before the high priest (Mt 26.63–64). It appears in the accounts of his baptism and transfiguration (Mk 1.11; 9.7). The Hebrews applied the phrase to heavenly beings (Job 38.7) and to a person who reflected the character of God. The Greeks referred to a divine being who remained on earth and devoted himself to the welfare of mankind as a "son of

God," the meaning that may have been intended by the centurion at the cross (Mk 15.39).

Son of Man   A phrase often used by Jesus (Mk 2.10; Lk 22.48). Though it occurs more than eighty times in the Gospels, it is seldom found elsewhere. Jesus may have used this title as an alternative to *Christ*, with its Messianic and nationalistic overtones, because it permitted him to introduce the idea of his coming suffering, a concept completely foreign to Jewish messianic hopes (Mk 8.31–33). In the Old Testament the phrase refers both to the people of Israel and the Messiah.

Teacher   The salutation of respect most often used in the Gospels by the disciples in addressing Jesus. As all learning among the Jews was associated with the Law, "teacher" had an exclusively religious connotation. The three interchangeable words, "teacher," "rabbi," and "master," occur some seventy times in the Gospels, indicating that the teachings of Jesus were widely regarded as authoritative (Lk 20.28; Mk 12.32). *See also* Master, Rabbi.

Word, The   The English translation of the Greek *Logos* denoting Jesus Christ in the prologue to the Gospel of John. This title, which appears also in Revelation 19.13, conveys the belief that he is the Son of God, as well as the Life and Light of men, and the Savior of the world, a belief that underlies the entire New Testament. "In the beginning was the Word, and the Word was with God, and the Word was God. . . . And the Word became flesh and dwelt among us" (Jn 1.1, 14). *Word* as applied to Christ is a development of the Old Testament concept of the Word of God as the creative activity of the Lord (Gen 1.3; Ps 33.6, 9), and as the means by which he made known his saving will to Israel through the prophets (Jer 1.4). *See also* Logos.

Other names and titles used by the early Christians to describe their Lord:

Advocate	1 Jn 2.1
Author of Life	Acts 3.15
Bread of Life	Jn 6.35
Cornerstone	Eph 2.20
Deliverer	Rom 11.26
Emmanuel, Immanuel ("God is with us")	Mt 1.23; cf. Isa 7.14
Good Shepherd or Great Shepherd	Jn 10.11; Heb 13.20
Guardian of Your Souls	1 Pet 2.25
High Priest	Heb 4.14
Holy One of God	Mk 1.24; Lk 4.34
Judge of the Living and the Dead	Acts 10.42
King of Kings	Rev 17.14
Lamb of God	Jn 1.29; Rev 5.6
Light of the World	Jn 8.12
Lord of Lords	Rev 17.14
Mediator of a New Covenant	Heb 9.15
Morning Star	Rev 22.16
Nazarene, The	Mt 2.23
Pioneer and Perfecter of our Faith	Heb 12.2
Power of God, The	1 Cor 1.24
Prince of Peace	Isa 9.6; cf. Jn 14.27
Prophet	Mt 21.11
Truth, The	Jn 14.6
Vine, The True	Jn 15.1
Wisdom of God, The	1 Cor 1.24

THE NAMES OF THE HOLY SPIRIT

Two groups of names denote the Holy Spirit in the English Bible. One group is centered around the word *Spirit;* the other includes various translations of the Greek *Parakletos.*

"Spirit" is the English rendering of the Hebrew *Ruach* and the Greek *Pneuma*, both of which originally indicated the "blowing" of the wind and the "breathing" of man. When the Old Testament *Ruach* refers to God, it is translated "Spirit." The Spirit is the agent of God's creative activity (Gen 1.2); it inspired Israel's rulers, prophets, and people (Judg 3.10; 1 Sam 10.10; Joel 2.28); it is omnipresent (Ps 139.7); and throughout the Old Testament it manifests God and acts on his behalf in his dealings with people. "I will put my Spirit within you, and you shall live," declared the Lord to the dry bones in Ezekiel's vision (Ezek 37.1–14). The Spirit is often explicitly named the Spirit of God (Ex 31.3) and the Spirit of the Lord (1 Sam 16.13).

In the New Testament, the Holy Spirit is God's presence and power in the individual person and the promise of life in "the world to come." The Holy Spirit figures in the stories of Jesus' birth (Lk 1.35), baptism (Mk 1.10), and temptation (Lk 4.1); and in the account of the descent of the Holy Spirit upon the apostles (Acts 2.1–4). The Spirit, known both as God's gracious power and equally as the presence of the Risen Christ (Rom 8.9), was called the Spirit of God and also the Spirit of Christ or the Spirit of Jesus Christ (Phil 1.19).

In Paul's benediction, "The grace of the Lord Jesus Christ and the love of God and the fellowship of the Holy Spirit be with you all" (2 Cor 13.14), and in the baptismal formula, "In the name of the Father and of the Son and of the Holy Spirit'' (Mt 28.19), we see the beginnings of the Church's concept of the Holy Spirit as the third person of the Trinity.

Although the King James Version generally translates *Pneuma* as ''Spirit,'' when the Greek word for ''Holy'' precedes *Pneuma*, this more than three-centuries-old version translates it with the obsolete term, ''Ghost,'' hence Holy Ghost.

The second name for the Holy Spirit is the Greek *Parakletos* 'helper,' 'advocate,' 'counselor,' 'intercessor.' In the farewell discourse of Jesus to his disciples, this Greek word in John 14.16, 26; 15.26; 16.7 is variously translated as: ''Advocate,'' in the New English Bible and the Jerusalem Bible; ''Comforter,'' in the King James Version; ''Counselor,'' in the Revised Standard Version; and ''Paraclete'' in the New American Version. In these passages from the Gospel of John, the Holy Spirit is also called the ''Spirit of Truth.'' In 1 John 2.1, Christ himself is called our ''advocate [*parakletos*] with the Father.''

VI
Familiar Phrases from the English Bible

The time-honored expressions listed below are among the most familiar Biblical phrases used by English-speaking people. Much of this phraseology was created by William Tyndale, but his successors, who produced the six English versions of the sixteenth century, added their own picturesque expressions and pungent, vigorous phrases. When the translators of the King James Version of 1611 gathered together this inherited wealth of expression and made their own contributions to it, they produced a superb English Bible. Its grace, simplicity, and felicitous phrases helped to form the language, endowing it with many of its characteristic turns of thought and making it an extraordinarily rich, flexible, and expressive vehicle for speech and writing.

The phrases below, except those marked "KJV," are from the Revised Standard Version, 1946–1952, which preserves intact most of the wording of the King James Version.

all things to all men	1 Cor 9.22
Am I my brother's keeper?	Gen 4.9
the apple of his eye	Deut 32.10

blind guides	Mt 15.14
bold as a lion	Prov 28.1
bottomless pit	Rev 9.1
built his house upon a rock	Mt 7.24
the burden and heat of the day	Mt 20.12, KJV
Cast your bread upon the waters	Eccles 11.1
like chaff before the wind	Ps 35.5
a cheerful giver	2 Cor 9.7
a citizen of no mean city	Acts 21.39
clay in the potter's hand	Jer 18.6
clean hands and a pure heart	Ps 24.4
clear as crystal	Rev 21.11
clothed and in his right mind	Mk 5.15
a cloud of witnesses	Heb 12.1
coals of fire	Ps 18.12
coat of many colors	Gen 37.3, KJV
crown of glory	1 Pet 5.4
crown of life	Rev 2.10
den of lions	Dan 6.7
den of thieves	Mt 21.13, KJV
down to the sea in ships	Ps 107.23
dust and ashes	Gen 18.27
of the earth, earthy	1 Cor 15.47, KJV
eat, drink, and be merry	Lk 12.19
the eleventh hour	Mt 20.9

the error of his way	Jas 5.20
every man's hand against him	Gen 16.12
An eye for an eye and a tooth for a tooth	Mt 5.38
faith as a grain of mustard seed	Mt 17.20
false prophets . . . in sheep's clothing	Mt 7.15
fat of the land	Gen 45.18
fatted calf	Lk 15.23
fear and trembling	Phil 2.12
feet . . . of clay	Dan 2.34
fought the good fight	2 Tim 4.7
the four corners of the earth	Isa 11.12
full of years	Gen 25.8
the gate of heaven	Gen 28.17
the gates of hell	Mt 16.18, KJV
Get behind me, Satan!	Mk 8.33
Gird up your loins	2 Kings 4.29
God save the king	1 Sam 10.24, KJV
good for nothing	Mt 5.13, KJV
goodly heritage	Ps 16.6
great possessions	Mk 10.22
green pastures	Ps 23.2
grinding the face of the poor	Isa 3.15
puts his hand to the plow	Lk 9.62
harden his heart	Ex 4.21

He who has ears to hear, let him hear	Mt 11.15
heap coals of fire on his head	Prov 25.22
heart's desire	Ps 21.2
hewers of wood and drawers of water	Josh 9.21
holier than thou	Isa 65.5, KJV
hope deferred	Prov 13.12
a house not made with hands	2 Cor 5.1
a house . . . divided against itself	Mk 3.25
How are the mighty fallen!	2 Sam 1.19
howling waste of the wilderness	Deut 32.10
inherit the wind	Prov 11.29, KJV
kick against the pricks	Acts 26.14, KJV
labor of love	1 Thess 1.3
the laborer is worthy of his hire	Lk 10.7, KJV
as a lamb to the slaughter	Isa 53.7, KJV
a land flowing with milk and honey	Ex 3.8
the last [will be] first	Mt 19.30
a law to themselves	Rom 2.14
length of days	Prov 3.2
let us reason together	Isa 1.18
lick the dust	Ps 72.9
make merry	Jer 30.19
Man shall not live by bread alone	Mt 4.4
a man after my heart	Acts 13.22

many are called, but few are chosen	Mt 22.14
the mark of the beast	Rev 19.20
the love of money is the root of all evils	1 Tim 6.10
out of the mouth of babes	Mt 21.16
a new heaven and a new earth	Rev 21.1
there is nothing new under the sun	Eccles 1.9
new wine into old wineskins	Mk 2.22
oil of gladness	Ps 45.7
outer darkness	Mt 8.12
out of the abundance of the heart the mouth speaks	Mt 12.34
at the parting of the way	Ezek 21.21
pearl of great price	Mt 13.46, KJV
pearls before swine	Mt 7.6
the powers that be	Rom 13.1, KJV
a very present help in trouble	Ps 46.1
Pride goes before destruction	Prov 16.18
prisoners of hope	Zech 9.12
a proud heart	Prov 21.4
the quick and the dead	1 Pet 4.5, KJV
the race is not to the swift	Eccles 9.11
ravenous wolves	Mt 7.15

reap the whirlwind	Hos 8.7
a reed shaken by the wind	Lk 7.24
a refuge in times of trouble	Ps 9.9, KJV
rejoiceth as a strong man to run a race	Ps 19.5, KJV
riotous living	Lk 15.13, KJV
rule them with a rod of iron	Rev 2.27
sackcloth and ashes	Mt 11.21
safe and sound	Lk 15.27
salt of the earth	Mt 5.13
see eye to eye	Isa 52.8, KJV
the seeing eye	Prov 20.12
sharp as a two-edged sword	Prov 5.4
like sheep for slaughter	Ps 44.11
sick unto death	2 Kings 20.1, KJV
signs of the times	Mt 16.3
escaped by the skin of my teeth	Job 19.20
slow to anger	Prov 16.32
smoother than butter	Ps 55.21
a soft answer	Prov 15.1
songs in the night	Job 35.10
sour grapes	Ezek 18.2
the spirit . . . is willing, but the flesh is weak	Mk 14.38
sticks closer than a brother	Prov 18.24
a still small voice	1 Kings 19.12

a stranger in a strange land	Ex 2.22, KJV
strength in the time of trouble	Ps 37.39, KJV
from strength to strength	Ps 84.7
suffer fools gladly	2 Cor 11.19, KJV
beat their swords into plowshares	Isa 2.4
as a tale that is told	Ps 90.9, KJV
teeth are set on edge	Ezek 18.2
tender mercies	Ps 25.6, KJV
terrible as an army with banners	Song 6.4
like a thief in the night	1 Thess 5.2
a thorn . . . in the flesh	2 Cor 12.7
in the twinkling of an eye	1 Cor 15.52
vain repetitions	Mt 6.7, KJV
valley of decision	Joel 3.14
vanity of vanities! All is vanity	Eccles 1.2
the voice of one crying in the wilderness	Mk 1.3
the wages of sin is death	Rom 6.23
wars and rumors of wars	Mt 24.6
as a watch in the night	Ps 90.4
grow weary in well-doing	Gal 6.9
weighed in the balances and found wanting	Dan 5.27
Well done, good and faithful servant	Mt 25.21
whited sepulchres	Mt 23.27, KJV

the wings of the wind	Ps 18.10
wise as serpents	Mt 10.16

VII
Quintessential Verses

In brief passages that embody the essential message of the books from Genesis to Revelation, this selection, compiled from many sources, introduces the reader to inexhaustible riches. Clearly, concisely, and in living words, these verses express the fundamental meaning of the Scriptures. The Bible is generous and inventive in communicating its faith, as quotations in subsequent volumes of this series demonstrate and as everyone from his or her personal reading will testify. The verses quoted below contain powerful words. Men and women have lived by them.

— — —

In the beginning God created the heavens and the earth. The earth was without form and void, and darkness was upon the face of the deep; and the Spirit of God was moving over the face of the waters. And God said, "Let there be light"; and there was light. And God saw that the light was good.

Genesis 1.1–4

Then God said, "Let us make man in our image, after our likeness. . . . So God created man in his own image, in the image of God he created him; male and female he created them. And God blessed them.

Genesis 1.26–28

Then the Lord said to Cain, "Where is Abel your brother?" He said, "I do not know; am I my brother's keeper?"

Genesis 4.9

Then Jacob awoke from his sleep and said, "Surely the Lord is in this place; and I did not know it. . . . How awesome is this place! This is none other than the house of God, and this is the gate of heaven."

Genesis 28.16–17

"The Lord watch between you and me, when we are absent one from the other."

Genesis 31.49

"You have seen . . . how I bore you on eagles' wings and brought you to myself. Now therefore, if you will obey my voice and keep my covenant, you shall be my own possession among all peoples . . . and you shall be to me a kingdom of priests and a holy nation."

Exodus 19.4–6

And God spoke all these words saying, "I am the Lord your God, who brought you out of the land of Egypt, out of the house of bondage.

"You shall have no other gods before me.
"You shall not make for yourself a graven image. . . .
"You shall not take the name of the Lord your God in vain. . . .
"Remember the sabbath day, to keep it holy. . . .

"Honor your father and your mother. . . .
"You shall not kill.
"You shall not commit adultery.
"You shall not steal.
"You shall not bear false witness against your neighbor.
"You shall not covet your neighbor's house . . . or
   anything that is your neighbor's."

Exodus 20.1–17

The Lord bless you and keep you:
The Lord make his face to shine upon
   you, and be gracious to you:
The Lord lift up his countenance upon
   you, and give you peace.

Numbers 6.24–26

Hear, O Israel: The Lord your God is one Lord; and you
shall love the Lord your God with all your heart, and with
all your soul, and with all your might.

Deuteronomy 6.4–5

Be strong and of good courage, do not fear or be in
dread of them: for it is the Lord your God who goes with
you; he will not fail you or forsake you.

Deuteronomy 31.6

The eternal God is your dwelling place,
   and underneath are the everlasting arms.

Deuteronomy 33.27

In peace I will both lie down and sleep;
   for thou alone, O Lord, makest me dwell in safety.

Psalm 4.8

When I look at thy heavens, the work of thy fingers,
   the moon and the stars which thou hast established;
what is man that thou art mindful of him,

and the son of man that thou dost care for him?
Yet thou hast made him little less than God,
   and dost crown him with glory and honor,

Psalm 8.3–5

O Lord, who shall sojourn in thy tent?
   Who shall dwell on thy holy hill?
He who walks blamelessly, and does what is right,
   and speaks truth from his heart;
who does not slander with his tongue,
   and does no evil to his friend. . . .

Psalm 15.1–3

The heavens are telling the glory of God;
   and the firmament proclaims his handiwork.

Psalm 19.1

Let the words of my mouth and the meditation
     of my heart be acceptable in thy sight,
   O Lord, my rock and my redeemer.

Psalm 19.14

The Lord is my shepherd, I shall not want;
   he makes me lie down in green pastures.
He leads me beside still waters;
   he restores my soul.
He leads me in the paths of righteousness
   for his name's sake.
Even though I walk through the valley of
     the shadow of death,
   I fear no evil;
for thou art with me;
   thy rod and thy staff,
   they comfort me.
. . .
Surely goodness and mercy shall follow me
   all the days of my life;

and I shall dwell in the house of the Lord
   for ever.

Psalm 23

Make me to know thy ways, O Lord;
   teach me thy paths.
Lead me in thy truth, and teach me,
   for thou art the God of my salvation;
   for thee I wait all the day long.

Psalm 25.4–5

The Lord is my light and my salvation;
   whom shall I fear?
The Lord is the stronghold of my life;
   of whom shall I be afraid?
. . .
I believe that I shall see the goodness of the Lord
   in the land of the living!
Wait for the Lord;
   be strong, and let your heart take courage;
   yea, wait for the Lord!

Psalm 27.1, 13–14

God is our refuge and strength,
   a very present help in trouble.
Therefore we will not fear though the earth should
      change,
   though the mountains shake in the heart of the sea;
though its waters roar and foam,
   though the mountains tremble with its tumult.

Psalm 46.1–3

Create in me a clean heart, O God,
   and put a new and right spirit within me.
Cast me not away from thy presence,
   and take not thy holy Spirit from me.

Psalm 51.10–11

Whom have I in heaven but thee?
   And there is nothing upon earth that I desire besides
      thee.
My flesh and my heart may fail,
   but God is the strength of my heart and my portion for
      ever.

Psalm 73.25–26

How lovely is thy dwelling place,
   O Lord of hosts!
My soul longs, yea, faints
   for the courts of the Lord;
my heart and flesh sing for joy
   to the living God.

Psalm 84.1–2

Lord, thou hast been our dwelling place
   in all generations.
Before the mountains were brought forth,
   or ever thou hadst formed the earth and the world,
   from everlasting to everlasting thou art God.

Psalm 90.1–2

He who dwells in the shelter of the Most High,
   who abides in the shadow of the Almighty,
will say to the Lord, "My refuge and my fortress;
   my God, in whom I trust."

Psalm 91.1–2

Know that the Lord is God!
   It is he that made us, and we are his;
we are his people, and the sheep of his pasture.

Psalm 100.3

The Lord is merciful and gracious,
   slow to anger and abounding in steadfast love.
He will not always chide,

nor will he keep his anger for ever.
He does not deal with us according to our sins,
  nor requite us according to our iniquities.
For as the heavens are high above the earth,
  so great is his steadfast love toward those who fear him.
                                                    Psalm 103.8–11

As a father pities his children,
  so the Lord pities those who fear him.
For he knows our frame;
  he remembers that we are dust.
As for man, his days are like grass;
  he flourishes like a flower of the field;
for the wind passes over it, and it is gone,
  and its place knows it no more.
But the steadfast love of the Lord is from everlasting to
      everlasting
  upon those who fear him,
  and his righteousness to children's children,
to those who keep his covenant
  and remember to do his commandments.
                                                    Psalm 103.13–18

The Lord will keep you from all evil;
  he will keep your life.
The Lord will keep
  your going out and your coming in
  from this time forth and for evermore.
                                                    Psalm 121.7–8

Unless the Lord builds the house,
  those who build it labor in vain.
                                                    Psalm 127.1

Behold how good and pleasant it is
  when brothers dwell in unity!
                                                    Psalm 133.1

Whither shall I go from thy Spirit?
   Or whither shall I flee from thy presence?
. . .
If I take the wings of the morning
   and dwell in the uttermost parts of the sea,
even there thy hand shall lead me,
   and thy right hand shall hold me.
If I say, ''Let only darkness cover me,
   and the light about me be night,''
even the darkness is not dark to thee,
   the night is bright as day;
   for darkness is as light with thee.

Psalm 139.7–12

Trust in the Lord with all your heart,
   and do not rely on your own insight.
In all your ways acknowledge him,
   and he will make straight your paths.

Proverbs 3.5–6

Pleasant words are like a honeycomb,
   sweetness to the soul and health to the body.

Proverbs 16.24

He who is slow to anger is better than the mighty,
   and he who rules his spirit than he who takes a city.

Proverbs 16.32

A cheerful heart is a good medicine,
   but a downcast spirit dries up the bones.

Proverbs 17.22

The people who walked in darkness
   have seen a great light;
those who dwelt in a land of deep darkness,
   on them has light shined.
. . .

For to us a child is born,
　　to us a son is given;
and the government will be upon his shoulder,
　　and his name will be called
"Wonderful Counselor, Mighty God,
　　Everlasting Father, Prince of Peace."
Of the increase of his government and of peace
　　there will be no end. . . .

　　　　　　　　　　　　　　　　　Isaiah 9.2, 6–7

Thou dost keep him in perfect peace,
　　whose mind is stayed on thee,
　　because he trusts in thee.

　　　　　　　　　　　　　　　　　Isaiah 26.3

Comfort, comfort my people,
　　says your God.
. . .
He will feed his flock like a shepherd,
　　he will gather the lambs in his arms,
he will carry them in his bosom,
　　and gently lead those that are with young.
. . .
He gives power to the faint,
　　and to him who has no might he increases strength.
Even youths shall faint and be weary,
　　and young men shall fall exhausted;
but they who wait for the Lord shall renew their strength,
　　they shall mount up with wings like eagles,
they shall run and not be weary,
　　they shall walk and not faint.

　　　　　　　　　　　　　　　　Isaiah 40.1,11,29–31

Fear not, for I am with you,
　　be not dismayed, for I am your God;

I will strengthen you, I will help you,
   I will uphold you with my victorious right hand.

Isaiah 41.10

"They ask of me. . . .
   'Why have we fasted, and thou seest it not?'
. . .
"Behold, in the day of your fast you seek your own
       pleasure,
   and oppress all your workers.
. . .
"Fasting like yours this day
   will not make your voice to be heard on high.
. . .
"Is not this the fast that I choose:
   to loose the bonds of wickedness,
   to undo the thongs of the yoke,
To let the oppressed go free,
   and to break every yoke?
Is it not to share your bread with the hungry,
   and bring the homeless poor into your house?"

Isaiah 58.3–4,6–7

Thus says the Lord: "Let not the wise man glory in his wisdom, let not the mighty man glory in his might, let not the rich man glory in his riches; but let him who glories glory in this, that he understands and knows me, that I am the Lord who practice steadfast love, justice, and righteousness in the earth; for in these things I delight, says the Lord."

Jeremiah 9.23–24

"Then you will call upon me and come and pray to me, and I will hear you. You will seek me and find me; when you seek me with all your heart, I will be found by you, says the Lord. . . ."

Jeremiah 29.12–14

A new heart I will give you, and a new spirit I will put within you; and I will take out of your flesh the heart of stone and give you a heart of flesh. And I will put my spirit within you, and cause you to walk in my statutes and be careful to observe my ordinances. . . . You shall be my people, and I will be your God."

Ezekiel 36.26–28

"I saw in the night visions,
and behold with the clouds of heaven
   there came one like a son of man,

. . .
And to him was given dominion
   and glory and kingdom,
that all peoples, nations, and languages
   should serve him;
his dominion is an everlasting dominion,
   which shall not pass away,
and his kingdom one
   that shall not be destroyed."

Daniel 7.13–14

When Israel was a child, I loved him,

. . .
Yet it was I who taught Ephraim to walk,
   I took them up in my arms;
   but they did not know that I healed them.
I led them with cords of compassion,
   with the bands of love.

Hosea 11.1,3–4

Seek good, and not evil,
   that you may live;
and so the Lord, the God of hosts, will be with you,
   as you have said.
Hate evil, and love good,
   and establish justice in the gate.

Amos 5.14–15

Woe to those who are at ease in Zion.
. . .
Woe to those who lie upon beds of ivory,
. . .
who drink wine in bowls,
    and anoint themselves with the finest oils,
    but are not grieved over the ruin of Joseph!"

Amos 6.1,4,6

He shall judge between many peoples,
    and shall decide for strong nations afar off;
and they shall beat their swords into plowshares,
    and their spears into pruning hooks;
nation shall not lift up sword against nation,
    neither shall they learn war any more;
but they shall sit every man under his vine and under his
        fig tree,
    and none shall make them afraid;
    for the mouth of the Lord of hosts has spoken.

Micah 4.3–4

He has showed you, O man, what is good;
    and what does the Lord require of you
but to do justice, and to love kindness,
    and to walk humbly with your God.

Micah 6.8

The righteous shall live by his faith.

Habakkuk 2.4

Not by might, nor by power, but by my Spirit,
    says the Lord of hosts.

Zechariah 4.6

Have we not all one father? Has not one God created us?
Malachi 2.10

But God created man for immortality, and made him in the image of his own eternal self.

> Apocrypha: Wisdom of Solomon 2.23, NEB

"Blessed are the poor in spirit, for theirs is the kingdom of heaven.

"Blessed are those who mourn, for they shall be comforted.

"Blessed are the meek, for they shall inherit the earth.

"Blessed are those who hunger and thirst for righteousness, for they shall be satisfied.

"Blessed are the merciful, for they shall obtain mercy.

"Blessed are the pure in heart, for they shall see God.

"Blessed are the peacemakers, for they shall be called sons of God.

"Blessed are those who are persecuted for righteousness' sake, for theirs is the kingdom of heaven."

> Matthew 5.3–10

"You are the light of the world. . . . Let your light so shine before men, that they may see your good works and give glory to your Father who is in heaven."

> Matthew 5.14,16

"You have heard that it was said, 'You shall love your neighbor and hate your enemy.' But I say to you, Love your enemies and pray for those who persecute you, so that you may be sons of your Father who is in heaven; for he makes his sun rise on the evil and on the good, and sends rain on the just and on the unjust."

> Matthew 5.43–45

"Pray then like this:
  Our Father who art in heaven,
  Hallowed be thy name.
  Thy kingdom come.

Thy will be done,
  On earth as it is in heaven.
Give us this day our daily bread;
And forgive us our debts,
  As we also have forgiven our debtors;
And lead us not into temptation,
  But deliver us from evil."

Matthew 6.9–13

"Do not lay up for yourselves treasures on earth, where moth and rust consume and where thieves break in and steal, but lay up for yourselves treasures in heaven. . . . For where your treasure is, there will your heart be also."

Matthew 6.19–21

"Ask, and it will be given you; seek, and you will find; knock, and it will be opened to you. For every one who asks receives, and he who seeks finds, and to him who knocks it will be opened."

Matthew 7.7–8

"Whatever you wish that men would do to you, do so to them; for this is the law and the prophets."

Matthew 7.12

"Come to me, all who labor and are heavy laden, and I will give you rest. Take my yoke upon you, and learn from me; for I am gentle and lowly in heart, and you will find rest for your souls. For my yoke is easy, and my burden is light."

Matthew 11.28–30

"For where two or three are gathered in my name, there am I in the midst of them."

Matthew 18.20

"I was hungry and you gave me food, I was thirsty and you gave me drink, I was a stranger and you welcomed me, I was naked and you clothed me, I was sick and you visited me, I was in prison and you came to me. . . . Truly, I say to you, as you did it to one of the least of these my brethren, you did it to me."

Matthew 25.35–36,40

"Go therefore and make disciples of all nations, baptizing them in the name of the Father and of the Son and of the Holy Spirit, teaching them to observe all that I have commanded you; and lo, I am with you always, to the close of the age."

Matthew 28.19–20

"Whoever does the will of God is my brother, and sister, and mother."

Mark 3.35

"If any man will come after me, let him deny himself and take up his cross and follow me. For whoever would save his life will lose it; and whoever loses his life for my sake and the gospel's will save it. For what does it profit a man, to gain the whole world and forfeit his life?"

Mark 8.34–36

And Jesus said to him, . . . "All things are possible to him who believes." Immediately the father of the child cried out and said, "I believe; help my unbelief!"

Mark 9.23–24

"With men it is impossible, but not with God; for all things are possible with God."

Mark 10.27

And one of the scribes . . . asked him, "Which commandment is the first of all?" Jesus answered, "The first is, 'Hear, O Israel: The Lord our God, the Lord is one; and you shall love the Lord your God with all your heart, and with all your soul, and with all your mind, and with all your strength.' The second is this, 'You shall love your neighbor as yourself.' There is no other commandment greater than these."

Mark 12.28–31

And the angel said to them, "Be not afraid; for behold, I bring you good news of a great joy which will come to all the people; for to you is born this day in the city of David a Savior, who is Christ the Lord. And this will be a sign for you: you will find a babe wrapped in swaddling cloths and lying in a manger." And suddenly there was with the angel a multitude of the heavenly host praising God and saying,

> "Glory to God in the highest,
> And on earth peace among men with whom he is
>   pleased!"

Luke 2.10–14

And he said to his disciples, "Therefore I tell you, do not be anxious about your life, what you shall eat, nor about your body, what you shall put on. For life is more than food, and the body more than clothing. . . . Consider the lilies, how they grow; they neither toil nor spin; yet I tell you, even Solomon in all his glory was not arrayed like one of these. But if God so clothes the grass which is alive in the field today and tomorrow is thrown into the oven, how much more will he clothe you, O men of little faith! And do not seek what you are to eat and what you are to drink, nor be of anxious mind. . . . Instead, seek his kingdom, and these things shall be yours as well.

"Fear not, little flock, for it is your Father's good pleasure to give you the kingdom."

Luke 12.22–23,27–29,31–32

And he . . . knelt down and prayed, "Father, if thou art willing, remove this cup from me; nevertheless not my will, but thine, be done."

Luke 22.41,42

And Jesus said, "Father, forgive them; for they know not what they do."

Luke 23.34

Then Jesus, crying with a loud voice, said, "Father, into thy hands I commit my spirit!" And having said this he breathed his last.

Luke 23.46

In the beginning was the Word, and the Word was with God, and the Word was God. He was in the beginning with God; all things were made through him, and without him was not anything made that was made. In him was life, and the life was the light of men. . . . And the Word became flesh and dwelt among us, full of grace and truth; we have beheld his glory, glory as of the only Son from the Father.

John 1.1–4,14

No one has ever seen God; the only Son, who is in the bosom of the Father, he has made him known.

John 1.18

For God so loved the world that he gave his only Son, that whoever believes in him should not perish but have eternal life.

John 3.16

"But the hour is coming, and now is, when the true worshipers will worship the Father in spirit and truth, for such the Father seeks to worship him. God is spirit, and those who worship him must worship in spirit and truth."

John 4.23–24

"I am the light of the world; he who follows me will not walk in darkness, but will have the light of life."

John 8.12

Jesus then said . . . "If you continue in my word, you are truly my disciples, and you will know the truth, and the truth will make you free."

John 8.31–32

"I came that they may have life, and have it abundantly."

John 10.10

"And I have other sheep, that are not of this fold; I must bring them also, and they will heed my voice. So there shall be one flock, one shepherd."

John 10.16

"A new commandment I give you, that you love one another; even as I have loved you, that you also love one another. By this all men will know that you are my disciples, if you have love for one another."

John 13.34–35

Jesus said to him, "I am the way, and the truth, and the life; no one comes to the Father, but by me. . . ."
Philip said to him, "Lord, show us the Father. . . ." Jesus said to him, "Have I been with you so long, and yet you do not know me, Philip? He who has seen me has seen the Father. . . ."

John 14.6,8–9

"These things I have spoken to you, while I am still with you. But the Counselor, the Holy Spirit, whom the Father will send in my name, he will teach you all things, and bring to your remembrance all that I have said to you."

John 14.25–26

"Peace I leave with you; my peace I give to you; not as the world gives do I give to you. Let not your hearts be troubled, neither let them be afraid."

John 14.27

"Abide in me, and I in you. As the branch cannot bear fruit by itself, unless it abides in the vine, neither can you, unless you abide in me."

John 15.4

"I have said this to you, that in me you may have peace. In the world you have tribulation; but be of good cheer, I have overcome the world."

John 16.33

"And this is eternal life, that they know thee the only true God, and Jesus Christ whom thou hast sent."

John 17.3

For the wages of sin is death, but the free gift of God is eternal life in Christ Jesus our Lord.

Romans 6.23

For all who are led by the Spirit of God are sons of God.

Romans 8.14

I consider that the sufferings of this present time are not worth comparing with the glory that is to be revealed to us.

Romans 8.18

We know that in everything God works for good with those who love him, who are called according to his purpose.

Romans 8.28

Who shall separate us from the love of Christ? Shall tribulation, or distress, or persecution, or famine, or nakedness, or peril, or sword?. . . No, in all these things we are more than conquerors through him who loved us. For I am sure that neither death, nor life, nor angels, nor principalities, nor things present, nor things to come . . . nor anything else in all creation, will be able to separate us from the love of God in Christ Jesus our Lord.

Romans 8.35–39

Do not be overcome by evil, but overcome evil with good.

Romans 12.21

May the God of hope fill you with all joy and peace in believing, so that by the power of the Holy Spirit you may abound in hope.

Romans 15.13

Do you not know that your body is a temple of the Holy Spirit within you, which you have from God? You are not your own; you were bought with a price. So glorify God in your body.

1 Corinthians 6.19–20

Now there are varieties of gifts, but the same Spirit; there are varieties of service, but the same Lord; and there are varieties of working, but it is the same God who inspires them all in every one. To each is given the manifestation of the Spirit for the common good.

1 Corinthians 12.4–7

If I speak in the tongues of men and of angels, but have not love, I am a noisy gong or a clanging cymbal. If I have prophetic powers, and understand all mysteries and all knowledge, and if I have all faith, so as to remove mountains, but have not love, I am nothing. . . .

Love is patient and kind; love is not jealous or boastful; it is not arrogant or rude. Love does not insist on its own way; it is not irritable or resentful; it does not rejoice at wrong, but rejoices in the right. Love bears all things, believes all things, hopes all things, endures all things.

Love never ends; as for prophecies, they will pass away; as for tongues, they will cease; as for knowledge, it will pass away. . . .

So faith, hope, love abide, these three; but the greatest of these is love.

1 Corinthians 13.1–2,4–8,13·

But in fact Christ has been raised from the dead, the first fruits of those who have fallen asleep. For as by a man came death, by a man has come also the resurrection of the dead. For as in Adam all die, so also in Christ shall all be made alive.

1 Corinthians 15.20–22

Where the spirit of the Lord is, there is freedom.
2 Corinthians 3.17

If any one is in Christ, he is a new creation.
2 Corinthians 5.17

God was in Christ reconciling the world to himself.
2 Corinthians 5.19

We are the temple of the living God. ·
2 Corinthians 6.16

A thorn was given me in the flesh. . . . Three times I besought the Lord about this, that it should leave me; but he said to me, "My grace is sufficient for you, for my power is made perfect in weakness."

2 Corinthians 12.7–9

In Christ Jesus you are all sons of God, through faith. For as many of you as were baptized into Christ have put on Christ. There is neither Jew nor Greek, there is neither slave nor free, there is neither male nor female; for you are all one in Christ Jesus.

Galatians 3.26–28

The fruit of the Spirit is love, joy, peace, patience, kindness, goodness, faithfulness, gentleness, self-control; against such there is no law.

Galatians 5.22–23

For by grace you have been saved through faith; and this is not your own doing, it is the gift of God—not because of works, lest any man should boast. For we are his workmanship, created in Christ Jesus for good works, which God prepared beforehand, that we should walk in them.

Ephesians 2.8–10

Let all bitterness and wrath and anger and clamor and slander be put away from you, with all malice, and be kind to one another, tenderhearted, forgiving one another, as God in Christ forgave you.

Ephesians 4.31–32

Finally, brethren, whatever is true, whatever is honorable, whatever is just, whatever is pure, whatever is lovely, whatever is gracious, if there is any excellence, if there is anything worthy of praise, think about these things.

Philippians 4.8

And let the peace of Christ rule in your hearts. . . . Let the word of Christ dwell in you richly. . . .

Colossians 3.15,16

God did not give us a spirit of timidity but a spirit of power and love and self-control.

2 Timothy 1.7

Now faith is the assurance of things hoped for, the conviction of things not seen. For by it the men of old received divine approval. By faith we understand that the world was created by the word of God, so that what is seen was made out of things which do not appear. . . . And without faith it is impossible to please him. For whoever would draw near to God must believe that he exists and that he rewards those who seek him.

Hebrews 11.1–3,6

But be doers of the word, and not hearers only, deceiving yourselves.

James 1.22

As each has received a gift, employ it for one another, as good stewards of God's varied grace.

1 Peter 4.10

Cast all your anxieties on him, for he cares about you.

1 Peter 5.7

If we say we have no sin, we deceive ourselves, and the truth is not in us. If we confess our sins, he is faithful and just, and will forgive our sins and cleanse us from all unrighteousness.

1 John 1.8–9

We know that we have passed out of death into life, because we love the brethren. He who does not love remains in death.

1 John 3.14

But if any one has the world's goods and sees his brother in need, yet closes his heart against him, how does God's love abide in him? Little children, let us not love in word or speech but in deed and in truth.

1 John 3.17–18

Beloved, let us love one another; for love is of God, and he who loves is born of God and knows God.

1 John 4.7

God is love, and he who abides in love abides in God, and God abides in him.

1 John 4.16

There is no fear in love, but perfect love casts out fear.
1 John 4.18

We love, because he first loved us.

1 John 4.19

"Behold, I stand at the door and knock; if any one hears my voice and opens the door, I will come in to him and eat with him, and he with me."

Revelation 3.20

And I heard a great voice from the throne saying, "Behold the dwelling of God is with men. He will dwell with them, and they shall be his people, and God himself will be with them; he will wipe away every tear from their eyes, and death shall be no more, neither shall there be mourning nor crying nor pain any more, for the former things have passed away."

And he who sat upon the throne said, "Behold, I make all things new. . . . To the thirsty I will give water without price from the fountain of the water of life. He who conquers shall have this heritage, and I will be his God and he shall be my son."

Revelation 21.3–7

SELECTED BIBLIOGRAPHY

Buttrick, George A., ed. *Interpreter's Dictionary of the Bible.* 4 vols. Nashville: Abingdon Press, 1962. A comprehensive, illustrated encyclopedia.

Cruden, Alexander. *Cruden's Concordance.* Edited by A.D. Adams and others. New York: Holt, Rinehart and Winston, 1939. Invaluable for use with the King James Version.

Ellison, John W. *Nelson's Complete Concordance of the Revised Standard Version.* New York: Thomas Nelson and Sons, 1957. Contains 310,000 word entries. About twenty-five hundred of these are included in the *Concise Concordance.* Thomas Nelson and Sons, 1959.

Hastings, James. *Dictionary of the Bible.* Revised edition, by Frederick C. Grant and H.H. Rowley. New York: Charles Scribner's Sons, 1963. A revision of a fifty-year-old, standard reference book.

Laymon, Charles M., ed. *The Interpreter's One-Volume Commentary on the Bible, Including the Apocrypha.* Nashville: Abingdon Press, 1971. A useful work of 1,386 pages by scholars of many faiths.

May, Herbert G.; Hunt, G.N.S.; and Hamilton, R.W., eds. *Oxford Bible Atlas.* 2d ed. London: Oxford University Press, 1974. Contains an illustrated history of the Biblical period, with maps and a gazeteer.

Miller, Madeleine S.; Miller, J. Lane. *Harper's Bible Dictionary.* 8th edition, revised by eminent authorities. New York: Harper and Row, 1973. A comprehensive, illustrated reference book with up-to-date archaeological information.

Neil, William. *Harper's Bible Commentary.* New York: Harper and Row, paperback edition, 1975. Readable and concise.

Price, Ira Maurice. *The Ancestry of our English Bible: An Account of Manuscripts, Texts, and Versions of the Bible.* 3d edition, revised by Wm. A. Erwin and Allen P. Wikgren. New York: Harper and Row, 1956. An authoritative account with fifty-three photographs and seven diagrams.

Young, Robert. *Analytical Concordance to the Bible.* Grand Rapids, Michigan: Wm. B. Eerdman's Publishing Co., 1955. 22d revised edition. An invaluable work that indicates the Hebrew, Aramaic, and Greek originals and distinguishes the various meanings underlying the words.

Index

Abraham, 4, 5
Aelfric, 33–34
Aids to Bible study, 27–28
Albright, William F., 6
Aldred's paraphrase, 33
Aldhelm, 32
Alfred, King, 33
American Bible Society, 53
American Standard Version, 47
Amos, 8
Anglo-Saxon (Old English) Gospels, 33
Anglo-Saxon (Old English) versions, 31–34
Anne Boleyn, 39–40
Apocalypse, 18
Apocrypha, 13–14
Apocryphal gospels and epistles, 19
Appearance of books: of New Testament, 15–16; of Old Testament, 9–11
Aramaic, 13, 25
Arrangement of books: of New Testament, 18; of Old Testament, 11–12
Arts and the Bible, 26–27
Athanasius, 18

Authorized Version, 40, 44–47, 48
Authorship of books, multiple, 8–9

Barker, Robert, 45
Bede, the Venerable, 31, 32
Ben Asher, 23
Bible, The: aids to study of, 27–28; aspects of, 1–3; historical value of, 5–7, 18; literary forms in, 2; name of (derivation), 10; preview of, 4–5; sequence of books of, 11–12, 18; theme of, 3; translations of, 24–25, 37–54; value of, 1
Bishops' Bible, 43, 45
Bodmer Papyri, 16
Book of Common Prayer, 5, 56, 57, 58
Bratcher, Robert G., 53
Byblos, 10

Caedmon, 31–32
Canon: definition of, 12; of New Testament, 16–18; of Old Testament, 13
Caxton, William, 37, 38

140